The Days *of* Not So Long Ago

Crystal A. Klimavicz

Charleston, South Carolina

Copyright © 2015 by **Crystal A. Klimavicz** (republished 2019)

All rights reserved. No part of this publication may be reproduced, distributed or transmitted in any form or by any means, without prior written permission. This book contains material protected under International and Federal Copyright Laws and Treaties. Any unauthorized reprint or use of this material is prohibited. No part of this book may be reproduced or transmitted in any form or by any means, electronic or mechanical, including photocopying, recording, or by any information storage and retrieval system without express written permission from the author/publisher.

Crystal A. Klimavicz

The Days of Not So Long Ago/ Crystal A. Klimavicz. – 2nd ed.

ISBN-978-1-941142-89-9

Note to the Reader

On my father's side of the family, there are twelve grandchildren and holiday gatherings were always held at my grandparent's house. Those times were noisy, fun and memorable, from the collective groans as we opened yet another pair of socks at Christmastime, to playing freeze tag during backyard barbecues on the Fourth of July. We ate baked beans, beef stew, French onion dip, apple squares, and lemon meringue pie; our get-togethers were almost always happy times.

The grandchildren were equally divided, six boys and six girls. I was the only one who talked to our grandfather and asked him about the past. I sat perched on the hassock at his feet and rattled off questions while the smoke from his dangling cigarette wafted in the air. His stories intrigued me and undoubtedly created the desire to eventually leave our small hometown.

To us, our grandfather was an easy-going and mild-mannered man. He had a quick and humorous wit as he sent verbal barbs to my grandmother, a woman who rarely smiled and puffed her own cigarettes in the easy chair beside him. He never raised his voice, despite the chaos of having five families converge in their small home.

It wasn't until years later that I would learn about his earlier days of heavy drinking and poker-playing, about suspected dalliances, his quick temper and a heavy hand on my father and his four siblings. All I knew of my grandfather was that he had lived an interesting life with captivating stories from across the Atlantic and home again. And I loved every minute of our talks.

My grandfather and grandmother have since passed away. With him, also went all those stories I heard. Stories that were never captured in writing, for I was too young at the time to know how special they were.

Fast-forward, thirty years later while volunteering at Summit Place, a nursing home on Daniel Island, South Carolina, and the importance of the past came to light. One afternoon, during a particularly competitive game of Hangman, some of the women in the room began talking about "the old war days," about rationing and blackout curtains, gas prices and pantyhose. Women in their eighties and nineties who sometimes couldn't remember which of the twenty-six letters of the alphabet the five vowels were, had a moving and enlightening conversation, while I listened with curious fascination.

In that moment, I knew that although I could no longer capture my own grandfather's life story, I would do so for others. I decided to interview some of the oldest people living there; people who understood my request and readily agreed to talk, and all were residents at Summit Place.

Some people, I knew from my weekly visits, while others I was introduced to. Everyone opened up and shared their life stories; stories that included death and loss, accidents and pain, love and joy, and all that comes with living on this Earth for nearly one hundred years.

I hope readers of their stories will enjoy them as much as the individuals enjoyed sharing. More importantly, I hope the collection will serve as a reminder to us all that the way the world is now, is not the way it's always been.

These are people who grew up during the Great Depression, a time of multiple wars in our nation's history. They saw civil rights at its worst and lived during a time when children had to walk for miles to school (yes, just as some of our parents used to lament) and spoke to adults only when spoken to. They were still simpler times, when people had little yet appreciated everything. Times when families stayed and worked together, with hope for an easier life for the next generation. These were hard-working people who endured and made American history.

Information and facts regarding places, companies, years, etc. was verified as much as possible. If it is not correct, may it gracefully be overlooked as the life stories themselves are the reason for this book. There is an old African proverb that says, "When an old man dies, a library burns," and resonates well with their stories. May you enjoy them all.

Crystal A. Klimavicz

Original publication edited by Angie Holleman and supported by the Daniel Island Historical Society. All photographs, including the front cover, are courtesy of Elizabeth Bush. Many thanks to you all for the help to get this project off the ground.

CONTRIBUTORS

Virginia "Ginny" (Marvin) Pfenninger - Pitsburgh, Pennsylvania

Louise (Goodwin) Clark - Sanford, North Carolina

Paul Richard Russell - Pittsburgh, Pennsylvania

Wanda (Locket) Brown - Anderson County, Tennessee

Katherine 'Kitty' (Asman) Proctor - Swansea, South Carolina

Betty (Martin) Rollings - Lonsdale, Tennessee

Lucille (Starnes) O'Connell - Birmingham, Alabama

James "Jim" Sexauer - Detroit, Michigan

Barbara (Dukes) Grant - Sumter, South Carolina

Anne (Graham) Raynes - Oklahoma City, Oklahoma

Robert "Bob" Elf - Jamestown, New York

Carolyn (Knuth) Matthews - Indianapolis, Indiana

Mabel (Joy) Ward - Williamsburg, South Carolina

Anthony "Tony" James - Richmond, Kentucky

Pittsburgh, Pennsylvania – August 1927

Virginia "Ginny" (Marvin) Pfenninger

Virginia Marvin was born in Pittsburgh, Pennsylvania in August of 1927 in the middle of the Prohibition era (1920 - 1933). Her parents, Genevieve and Nicholas, emigrated to Pennsylvania decades before like many others from Great Britain and Europe. The city of Pittsburgh has experienced a variety of reputations over the years, first from the influx of immigrants, to later being a nationally recognized maker of steel and iron, then as a hotbed of bootlegging and alcoholic consumption during the riotous Prohibition years.

Ginny had two older brothers, Hank and Ray, with about two years between each of the siblings. Their father, Nicholas, served as the paymaster for a local manufacturing company and worked long hours on the job. Their mother, Genevieve, was a wonderful cook, and all three children always looked forward to their mother's home-cooked meals. "As did half the neighborhood," Ginny joked with a twinkle in her eye. She recalled this about those early childhood days at home with family:

"My father was always dressed in a white shirt; I don't think I ever saw him wear anything else. He was a good man who worked hard, but it was mother who did everything around the house. And after every meal, daddy would sit back, pat his stomach and say, 'Thank you, Mother, that was the best meal I ever had.' He always acknowledged her for what she did.

"My mother was a sweet woman. If someone mentioned that it was their birthday, she would buy them a card or bake something special. She was a wonderful baker. Her favorites were Christmas (fruit) cakes and Punch Cakes. Punschkrapfen or Punschkrapferl (punch cake, a classic Austrian confection of pastry with a nice rum flavor, similar to the petit fours, a French pastry). Her real specialty, though, was pies. She made apple, rhubarb, and blueberry pies… they were all delicious."

The local school the three Marvin children attended was St. Mary of the Assumption Parish, the same place the family attended church. Founded in 1842, the origin of parishes can be traced back to the arrival of German immigrants in Pittsburgh, primarily farmers and laborers. A typical Catholic parochial school, Jenny had this to say: "We never did anything without praying about it first. And the teachers were very strict, we didn't dare get out of line, not ever."

Growing up, Ginny and her two brothers spent much of their time outdoors, and the boys looked after Ginny, protecting their 'baby sister.' When the kids were old enough, they and their friends took buses everywhere to get around town: to the swimming pool, ice-skating rink, and even to the theater.

Ginny loved the live performances, especially *West Side Story*: an American musical, book by Arthur Laurents and music by Leonard Bernstein, inspired by William Shakespeare's play, *Romeo and Juliet*. She said, even if she saw the show a hundred times, she'd never tire of watching it.

When she was just thirteen, Ginny started dating a local boy, Paul Davis. They continued to date until he went off to war. When he returned, they decided to go their separate ways. One of her brothers, Hank, was kept a Prisoner of War (POW) during WWII and spent two long years in a German prison camp. He did survive the ordeal and eventually returned to the United States, as well.

Ginny was socially involved in many activities during high school. She served as Vice President of her class and as an active member of the Yearbook committee. She graduated at the age of seventeen, the year was 1945, and upon graduation she took a job in a dress store as a sales associate. After a year, she decided to serve as a nurses' aid at the Miles Brian High School.

It was during this time when she met her future husband, Joe Pfenninger, at the famed West View Park Danceland music hall in Pittsburgh. For sixty years, Danceland was a fun, local venue that brought in the best of the top performers, including the Beatles and the Rolling Stones. West View was a favorite place to dance to the music of the big bands and the latest hit songs until it closed its doors in 1989. The night the two met, Ginny was dancing when one of Joe's friends introduced them.

> "Joe wasn't the best dancer", she said with a sweet smile, "but he was persistent, I'll give him that. He kept asking me to dance, again and again."

Ginny and Joe Pfenninger began dating, and she soon learned of his love for planes, for Joe had always wanted to learn how to fly. He was a few years older than she and had already served in the Air Force in WWII and returned home by the time they met. He worked his way up to becoming a lieutenant pilot, which was quite an accomplishment in those days.

He never actually saw active duty in the war, though, for it ended just as his training program completed. He did have a close call flying drills over Texas one day when he and his group became lost in a major storm. After a few perilous hours, they were able to find their way back to the base. A picture of Joe proudly standing in front of his plane is one of Ginny's cherished photos.

By the time the two met at the West View dance hall, Joe had already settled into civilian life and purchased a local foundry. A foundry is a factory which produces metal castings; metals are cast into shapes by melting them into a liquid, pouring the metal in a mold, and removing the mold material or casting after the metal has solidified as it cools. Joe managed and ran the foundry and worked hard.

Reserved in some ways, Joe a nice guy whom all the other girls thought was 'cute.' He loved to watch sports, baseball and football, in particular. One season, he got the opportunity to throw some pitches in a Pittsburgh city league playoff game, broadcasted on the local radio station. Ginny and Joe dated for five years before he proposed to her. Everyone always told Ginny what a lucky girl she was, and they were soon married right at her family church, St. Mary's Parish.

> "As owner of the foundry, Joe was a dedicated employer who worked harder as the years went by. And though he was usually there

six days a week, he never brought his problems home with him.

> "One of Joe's proudest moments was being elected president of the Smaller Manufactures Council, when he was invited to the White House with then-president Jimmy Carter. They asked him to discuss the manufacturing concerns for the city of Pittsburgh. 'I just hope I made a good impression of myself and the city', Joe said with a grin when he returned home."

During this time, Ginny worked as a bank teller in McKees Rocks, Pennsylvania. The intersection of McKees Rocks, Pittsburgh and Allegheny was an area known as the 'Bottoms'; a neighborhood which is also the site of the McKees Rocks Indian Mound, a designated historic landmark where the oldest human bones in eastern North America have been discovered.

Yet once their first child came along, she had to leave the bank, for in those days women didn't work once they started showing. Her life was spent being a wonderful mother at home raising their children. Together, Ginny and Joe had four children, and all boys: Mark, Joe, David and Jeff. This is what Ginny recalls of life during those early days:

> "I was always running the boys around town for sports, music lessons, and after-school activities. And just as it was at my parents' house when I grew up, our house became the center of attention in the neighborhood for the

local kids. Our boys had their friends over, and it seemed like I made meals day-in and day-out for them all.

"I have to say, though, that I liked it best when the kids were still at home with us. But I was also guilty of trying to give my kids everything they wanted, even when I knew I shouldn't. We all worked hard in those days, really hard, and I know that Joe and I did our best for our children."

Their son, Joe, had this to add about the popularity of his childhood home during those early years:

"We had the biggest, best yard in the neighborhood, with a great tree house and large sandbox in the back. My mom was always making meals for the kids, just like her mother before her. Our house was constantly full of people, and I have great memories of everyone there together."

Years later, after the boys were all grown and had left home, Ginny went back to work. She took a job as a receptionist at nearby Allegheny General Hospital. Allegheny opened its doors back in 1885, with modest facilities and medical resources. The hospital evolved from fifty beds inside of two adjoining brick homes into one of the country's premier health-care institutions. The facility is a national leader in cancer, cardiovascular, neuroscience, and orthopedic and rehabilitation care, and Ginny worked there until the day she would retire.

Of the couples' four children, Jeff lives near his childhood home in Pittsburgh and flips houses for a living; he is also the lead singer and guitar player for a Rolling Stones cover band. The band, Mother's Little Helpers, was the dream child of Jeff whose love for both music and the Stones' music inspired the band's creation.

Mark, the second son, worked in their father's foundry and machine shop, then after the business closed down, he worked for a few different businesses keeping machinery and trucks in working order.

Son David worked in the stagehand's union and did lighting for concerts and various theater performances in Pittsburgh, though he passed away three years before.

And Joe and his wife Kelly have two children, Paige and Claire; they live nearby on Daniel Island. Ginny's husband Joe has passed away; she lives at Summit Place on Daniel Island, South Carolina and had this to say about her life: "It's just so nice to be in such a beautiful area, with so many friendly people and family to enjoy it with. I am truly blessed."

Savannah, Georgia - March 1921

Minnie Ruth (Spell) Fontenot

'Minnie' Ruth (Spell) Fontenot was born in Savannah, Georgia in 1932. She enjoyed a wonderful, selfless life, one centered on a passion for playing music and on her family, and she was committed to them both. When asked about those days, she gave an immediate response and grinned:

> "I've had a good life because all of it was so happy. I got to do the things I wanted. I

wanted to sing, play the guitar, and have a family. That's what I did, and it was all good."

As a child, she grew up with nine brothers and sisters on the outskirts of town. They lived on Perry Street in Savannah, then later on moved into a bigger house as the family grew. The home was also located closer to both town and the children's schools.

One of Minnie's fonder memories was going to the ice-skating rink with friends. She recalls one particular night when a young man continued to skate around and around her until she finally asked him what he was doing. She teased him, said if he didn't stop, he'd make her fall. The man smiled and told her he'd catch her if he did. The two were soon talking and laughing, and that night became the first date of many the couple would share together. Minnie and Louis Anthony Fontenot, or Tony as she called him, were married six months later, a few months after Minnie turned nineteen, as typical of couples during that era.

Tony was in the Air Force at the time, and within a year after they married, he was stationed at the Air Force base in Puerto Rico. They lived there for three years, where Minnie had two of their three children. Of their time in Puerto Rico, she said she learned only a few Spanish words, "Really, just enough to get by," and admitted that she was always too busy with the children to do much more.

After Tony's Puerto Rico assignment, he was stationed back in Savannah and while on TDY (temporary duty) he was sent off to England in 1955, then to Japan and finally to Germany. When Tony returned from, he didn't talk about his experience overseas. He did, however, say he liked Germany best, and when he retired from the army, he sought a German company to work for—Robert Bosch. He remained there for the rest of his working days. However, Minnie always felt like her mother before her, that her first place was in the home, taking care of children.

> "I was employed in a few different places, stores like Montgomery Ward, but we moved around so much, and I had enough to do at home, so I never really made anything of it."

Beyond Minnie's family life, there has always been an equal passion for something else in her heart, and that was music. For Minnie Ruth Fontenot is an accomplished woman who once sang, played guitar, and performed on many Southern stages with a love for music that was equaled by her talent. She learned to play guitar when she was ten years old and practiced for hours each day to perfect her craft; she grew to enjoy every minute of being on stage entertaining audiences and made quite a name for herself.

At fourteen, she started performing in small public venues around Savannah, churches and town festivals. Around the time, a girlfriend encouraged her to enter the 'Ms. Savannah' contest as a model contestant (Minnie chuckled, said she had the legs for it back then). However, when she walked on stage, she saw the Mayor's daughter had also entered the contest and was standing there, "preening like a peacock".

Without malice or regret, Minnie relayed the outcome of that contest. "Sure enough, the Mayor's daughter won." She expressed no bitterness about the disappointment. "That's the way things are sometimes done." However, Minnie would experience this same lack of fairness a few times in her life.

After she started singing outside of the home and word spread about her musical abilities, Minnie quickly garnered a following. She sang pop and country, old folk songs and hymns, and the requests for her performances quickly rose. By the age of fifteen, she had been invited to sing on numerous stages in town. Some of the hymns audiences repeatedly asked Minnie to sing were *Amazing Grace*, *Mama's Not Dead She's only Asleepin'*, and *How Great Thou Are*, and she loved them all.

One day, she met another singer, Betty Lanier, and together the two girls found a band to join. The band was called the Boys of the West and was made up of rhythm guitar, bass guitar, steel guitar ("They don't play those anymore, though." *), drums and piano. Yet soon after the band members left, Minnie and Betty formed their own group, The Barnyard Sweethearts. Betty was a few years older than Minnie, it was Betty and her mother who took the young women to most of these events. Minnie's father worked many hours to support his family and her mother was busy at home taking care of all of the other children.

The Barnyard Sweethearts sang at weddings, church events, fairs and festivals, and were "in demand every weekend." Minnie and Betty even sang in the beautiful Avon Theater in Savannah (opened in 1944 and eventually closed its doors in 1970; it's now the location of a Japanese restaurant). The girls were even invited to sing on the radio, where their voices were broadcast well beyond her the streets of their hometown.

When Minnie turned seventeen, a manager from Nashville had come to town to hear her and approached her at a show. "He said he liked what he'd heard and invited me to come to Nashville with him to try to make it big." Minnie was elated. However, her father intervened and forbade her to go. Her parents didn't play any music and said pursuing a career in something so frivolous when there was work to be done at home. Minnie Fontenot had talent and could have perhaps become a well-known name in the country music business had circumstances been different.

> "My daddy didn't let me go after my dreams, and my mother always just went along with whatever he said. They were so old-fashioned and yes, I was upset, but they were the sweetest parents you could have. My brothers and sister and I, we were good children, and we just did whatever they asked us."

During her senior year of high school, Minnie met a piano player named Lefty Prizell and another young, female singer. She asked Minnie to sing with her in a high-class nightclub in Savannah. Minnie sang there a few times, though eventually she stopped because she felt uncomfortable in such an adult venue without a mentor behind her or the support of her parents.

Soon after this period of her life, Minnie met Tony at the local skating rink and not long after, the two were married. Between moving to Puerto Rico, the start of her own family, and following Tony's career in the Air Force, those circumstances all proved to be the end of Minnie's musical career and the chance to make it big. However, neither her passion for or involvement with music ended there.

Although Minnie may have stopped singing on stage herself, one day she saw a young girl at a festival who was performing and showed "real potential". Minnie remembers their first meeting with great fondness. "I asked her as soon as we met if she wanted to be a star. The girl said yes with the brightest brown eyes, she was just beautiful." The girl was Angie Raley, she was twelve years old at the time, and people already loved to hear her sing even at such a young age.

With Angie's agreement, Minnie and her husband took on the role as the girl's manager. They booked her shows and took her to everyone. They never let Angie out of their sight, and Minnie laughed remembering that she even went to the ladies' room with her, so the young girl wasn't left alone. People clamored for miles to catch Angie's performances. The band that played with Angie was paid $500 for each gig, but Minnie told the venues that Angie would have to get $100 of that money for being the star of the show.

"You see, her family didn't have much at all, so I made sure we took care of her. I took Angie shopping and got her new clothes because she didn't have anything, really, before she'd started signing. I did everything for her."

The first place Angie sang for-pay under the management of Minnie and Tony was on stage in Summerville, South Carolina at the venue, "Our Place". The second location was at the MCO Club at the Air Force Base in North Charleston. Angie continued to receive requests at different venues as her popularity increased, and together they went to them all. In 1987, there was a singing contest in Charleston where Angie won Ms. Country.

After Angie won this contest and made the press, Minnie and Tony took her to Nashville to meet with a record company. Minnie expected Angie to have the opportunity to make her first record there, yet she retells this about the disheartening experience:

> "I'd already given those record people $100, but when we got there, there was another girl they'd decided on, before we even walked through the door. I just couldn't believe it.
>
> "We were really hoping for a chance, maybe even to win the $10,000 grand prize, but they'd already chosen who they wanted, and we went away with nothing, just like the beauty pageant with the Mayor's daughter years before."

Through the years when Minnie and her husband managed Angie's career, they never asked for a dime. They helped Angie build a following and tried to make her a star. Minnie said her own children may have been jealous of Angie, who also called Minnie, "Mom", and Tony, "Dad".

But Angie had essentially grown up with them, and Minnie looked at the young girl as family. She and Tony gave Angie everything they could until the girl's parents stepped in and took over all that she and Tony had done. By then, Angie had started paying more attention to boys than to her career and had almost stopped coming to practices and music gigs altogether, anyway.

Despite her own music career that did not have the chance to take off, and the attempt to help make Angie a star, Minnie looks back on her life with fondness and has a scrapbook full of articles and photos of Angie and her singing engagements.

During her own numerous visits to Nashville, Minnie had the opportunity to meet country pop stars including Reba McIntyre, Dolly Parton and Ernest Tubbs. She has autographed pictures from Alabama, Hank Williams (who was her husband's good friend), Garth Brooks, and Ronnie Milsap—pictures now kept in other dust-covered photo albums sitting atop her dresser. She said this about her life, with a sweet faraway look in her eyes:

"I've met so many great people, I can't remember them all now. I'm afraid I can't sing anymore like that, but I still love music. And I lost touch with Angie and have no idea where she is now, but if she's out there somewhere, I'd love to see her again, I really would."

As for her nine siblings, Minnie has one sister who lives in Savannah and suffers from Alzheimer's disease, and one who lives in Summerville still living in her home. All but brother is gone; he also stayed in Savannah, in a home similar to Summit Place. When asked about seeing him or others in her family, her matter-of-fact response was swift, "Oh, I'd love to see them all, but I just can't get there anymore", then she patted at her legs that now rest in the wheelchair she needs to move around.

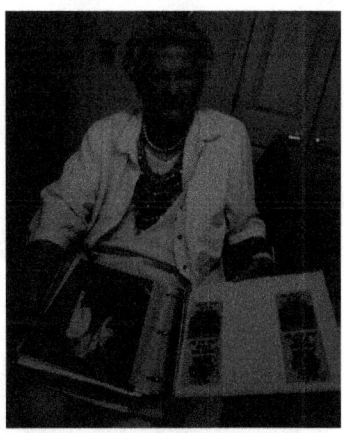

Minnie was married to Tony for sixty years until he passed away, eleven years ago. Of their three children, her only remaining living child is daughter, Diana, who lives in Hanahan, South Carolina. Daughter, Linda, died from cancer, and son, David, had problems with his heart, though the exact nature of his ailment is uncertain to her. She has two grandchildren and two great-grandchildren who live in Tennessee, five grandchildren and three great-grandchildren in Charleston.

> "After my son David passed, the doctors explained it all to me, but they used so many big words, I didn't know what it was that finally took him. David worked for years as a car salesman and was very good with people."

Then she added with small laugh, "But it's still a wonderful life," referring to the annual Christmas television show of the man, played by James Stewart, who was shown the beauty of life by seeing what the world would have been had he not been there.... a lovely reminder for us all from a woman who didn't fulfill her dreams, yet still looks back on life with love.

* *"The steel guitar used to be an instrument, but now refers to a sound, especially in country music. Nowadays, folks will play their electric guitars on their laps and use a slide to get the same effect as the old steel guitar instrument."*

Sanford, North Carolina − April 1924

Louise (Goodwin) Clark

Louise Goodwin was born in Sanford, North Carolina in April of 1924. Though there was initial speculation that her ancestors may have been descendants of the famous Captain Goodwin who landed on Plymouth Rock in 1620, no one confirmed the family myth. When Louise was older, her father told her that more than likely their family line sailed to the America's during the time of the potato famine in Ireland, around 1845.

Her father, Caleb Walker Goodwin, worked as a foreman in the local mills during Louise' early childhood years. He had to relocate his family often as he was transferred from one mill to the next. They first moved from Sanford to Raleigh when Louise was two years old, then to Durham when she was four, and finally out to the country when she was in the second grade.

In Durham, her father ran a store which had a filling station in the front. Yet the opportunity was ill-timed, for it was during the Great Depression from 1929 - 1939, when people could no longer pay their bills or even buy gas. He had no choice but to close the shop, move his family, and start over.

> "I remember when my daddy owned the store and the filling station, he'd give me a big bag of candy to eat. Then I'd go back home, sneak behind our house and hide up in a tree. I wanted all the candy to myself, and I didn't want to share it with any of her kids. It was not a pleasant situation living with her, but I still had a good childhood and I loved my family."

Their last family move occurred when Louise was seven. Her father turned to farming then and started a large farm about six miles outside of Durham, in a little country town called Oak Grove. He raised tobacco during the summer, and corn, sweet potatoes and tomatoes during the off season. The family remained in Oak Grove, North Carolina for the remainder of her childhood. Yet it was their first family move to Raleigh that had involved a major life event change for the Goodwin family and was a tragic one.

Louise's mother Lula Magnolia, or Maggie as she was called, passed away while giving birth to Louise's youngest brother. Louise was just two years old, and though she doesn't remember her mother, she said with fondness that people would always describe Maggie as 'a sweet woman, just like her'.

Louise had her brother, twin brothers plus two other older brothers, and an elder sister by eight years. Her oldest brothers helped take care of the family, the twins worked on the farm, and the older sister took on the role of 'mother' after Maggie passed. A picture of her mother, adorned in hat and petticoat, sits on Louise's bedroom shelf. Louise remembers this about those early years:

> "When my daddy was a foreman in the hosiery mill, and I was real little, my sister would throw me into this huge box full of socks there. Oh, I used to love that, I'd laugh so hard every time. Even though our mother was gone and that was terrible, we had each other, and it was enough."

After their mother passed away, Louise's baby brother was sent to live with his grandmother and aunt in Raleigh. There he stayed for his childhood, away from his father and siblings. The women had requested Louise, as well, but her father refused to let her go. He only allowed the baby to go because he knew he couldn't properly take care of an infant, alone.

Louise recalls that some of her most cherished childhood memories were the times her younger brother came to stay with them and during the visits she made to Raleigh to see him. She recalled going to the parks in the big city, with the animals to ride on, foods and treats, and other exciting opportunities. This was the first time in her life she'd ever seen a merry-go-round, and memories of those summer visits stayed.

One year after Louise's mother's death, her father remarried a serious and rather aloof woman named Anna Dora. Together, he and Anna Dora had four more children over the next eight years. Louise said her stepmother took great pains to keep her own children separate from Louise and her siblings. Anna Dora did not often allow her children to play with them, and she even had her own children sleep all together in another room away from Louise and her siblings.

Louise was as close to Dora's children as she could be, given the limitations the woman imposed upon everyone. However, once she left home, neither Louise nor her brothers or sister hardly ever saw Dora or their half brothers and sisters again.

She recalled her high school days as some of her fondest. She loved sports, particularly playing basketball as a guard, as well as softball as a pitcher. She was quite good at them both, and in her senior year she was voted 'Most Athletic Female' in her graduating class.

She laughed, remembering how the school administration didn't allow her to wear her basketball uniform on stage when she went up to accept her award. They said it was too short for public display, not 'befitting' for a young lady. Instead, they made her put on a tennis outfit on with a cute but longer skirt. Then a teacher stuck a tennis racket in her hand just before she went up to accept the award. The irony was that Louise "couldn't play tennis for beans" as all the students knew and laughed right along with her during the presentation.

Her aunt, the one who helped raise her younger brother, gave Louise her own daughter's clothes after she'd outgrown them. These homemade clothes were the "in" style back then with pants and a matching shirt.

"I was so proud when I stood at the blackboard at school wearing those outfits, because they weren't like the clothes my stepmother made and handed down to me. Those were ugly and the hems were far too long, even in those days. My aunt's handmade clothes were in style, and I felt like a million bucks wearing them."

She recalled with a smile how one night she had been playing in a basketball game and one of her brothers (who ended up going to seminary school to become a minister) was standing next to a young man whom Louise had previously dated. The guy, not knowing who her brother was, leaned over and said, "You see that girl over there (pointing to Louise), she's an angel, a real angel." My brother snorted and responded, 'She's no angel, I'll tell you, she's my sister!', and he shooed the guy away.

"Yes, my brothers loved me and took good care of me. They all did after our mother had died, but we had to look out for each other."

Another humorous story from Louise's childhood involved the same brother who would later become a minister, and he tried to teach Louise how to play the guitar. She was about nine then and remembers having blisters on her fingers from practicing.

Their father had an old mule he plowed with, and the kids would sometimes ride the mule around the farm. Louise tried to get on it one day to play her guitar because she wanted to look like the people she'd seen in the movies. But the mule bucked her off, and she landed in the bushes.

"I didn't get hurt, but my brother laughed so hard I thought he was going to split himself in two. He was the one with talent and had a beautiful singing voice. He would go by the radio station every day on his way back from school and sing songs on the radio there. Everyone loved his voice, I know.

"Then one day, he brought me along, and they asked me to sing so I sang the only song I knew, 'Goody Goody'. It wasn't a great performance, and they never asked me back. But I got to sing, all the same."

The year was 1943 when Louise graduated from high school, two years before WWII had officially ended. She'd always thought she would become a nurse after, said she even "put that occupation down" when asked what her plans were after graduation. She never applied to become one, though, and instead went to live with her sister in Winston-Salem for the remainder of the war.

There, she secured a job working at a war plant on the assembly line. The plant was located on the outskirts of town and employed hundreds of women. There were just a few male foremen who ran the plant, those who couldn't go to war to fight for medical or physical reasons. "One was a good-looking man who liked to cozy up to the girls and hug them whenever he could. He was married, though, and harmless."

Louise tried to play basketball while she worked at the plant. The other players were taller, though, so she sat on the bench and eventually stopped playing. One day, the actor Cesar Romero visited the plant to give the women a rallying speech; he was serving in the Coast Guard at the time. "When he thanked us for what we were doing, the girls swooned." It's interesting to note that none of the plant workers ever knew what exactly they were making or working on. Not until years later, did she discover they had been building batteries for ships to signal to one another during the war.

She made a number of good friends during the years she worked at the plant. For many years, she kept in touch with them. Two women in particular were sisters, Anne and Blanche Adams, and became her closest friends, and their parents were very good to Louise, as well. "They took me right in as if I was one of their own," she recalls.

The Adams women were Rainbow Girls and invited Louise to the club's many meetings and banquets. The International Order of the Rainbow for Girls is a Masonic youth service organization which teaches leadership training through community service for girls, ages eleven through twenty-one. They learn the value of charity through work with local and Grand (state or country) service projects. Some controversial aspects of the organization included its compatibility with the teachings of Christianity; today the Girl Scout Organization is more popular in U.S. communities.

After the war ended and Louise left her job at the plant, she took a job working for the local telephone company. This is where she met her future husband, Chevis Clark. He was with Weston Electric from Charleston, where he lived then, and had visited Winston-Salem on a work assignment. She was working at the switchboard and said she looked up to see him, "staring and smiling at me like a fool." Chevis asked her out that very day. They went together for about six months and soon were married; Louise was twenty-years old.

Chevis was an artist and went on to study at the Art School in Atlanta, Georgia, in the High Museum. Though he had a GI bill from the Navy (a law providing a range of benefits for World War II veterans) to help pay for part of his schooling, Louise worked the switchboard at Southern Bell during the time he studied in school to support them and his studies.

Chevis had completed three years of schooling, when the couple had to unexpectantly move out-of-state at his parent's request. Unfortunately for Louise, she had just received a promotion to Supervisor *and* was already pregnant with the couple's first child. Despite the inconvenient timing, the couple left Atlanta and dutifully moved to Jacksonville to be near his family. However, they soon learned that Chevis' mother had lied by telling the young couple Chevis' father had a heart problem just so they would come to Jacksonville.

> "I was so mad at the time, but it didn't matter in the end because not long after, we left Florida and move to Charleston, and that's where we stayed."

Following the couple's move to Charleston, Chevis went on to teach art with Ray Goodbread at the Gibbes Art Gallery School and at various studios downtown. Over the years, his art which mostly consisting of works in the watercolor medium, won 1st, 2nd, and 3rd place in the Carolina Art Association and the Guild of South Carolina Artists state exhibitions. He's also a founding member of the distinguished group, the Charleston Art Guild. '

Though Chevis' career did well through the years, after twenty-five years of marriage, and after the kids had all left home, Louise and her husband amicably agreed to go their separate ways. Chevis had met a student from art school, the couple fell in love and he eventually married her. Despite the unfortunate circumstances, Louise admitted that she liked the woman very much and spoke fondly of her. She said artists are just different from non-artistic people, and not like the rest.

"Really, I think they should marry their own kind. Artists are a unique group and they seem to understand each other better, that's all I can say."

Besides an old family friend, Louise never had another love interest, nor did she remarry. The daughter of Chevis' sister-in-law Patricia (Pat), Cheryl, continues to keep Louise and her children involved with his side of the family to this day. Pat was close friends with Mark Clark, after which the Mark Clark Expressway also known as Interstate 526 (I-526) is named.

Mark was a top commander in the Army in WWI and though he had a somewhat controversial career, he received many medals for his service. A movie was made about him in 1968 called The Devil's Brigade with William Holden in the lead role. Louise has a picture of her sister-in-law sitting next to Mark Clark at a dinner function. She said when her children were young and Mark's picture was in the paper, her children would point and say "Granddaddy" because he looked so much like their own grandfather.

While they were married, Louise and Chevis had four children: three sons and a daughter. Chevis, Jr., the oldest son, is a gemologist in downtown Charleston, at Sohn & McClure Jewelers. As a child, he played the drums with a strong aptitude for music, showing his own artistic talents in the family. David, the couple's middle son, was a curator on the Yorktown ship.

Like his father, he is a very talented artist, and his pictures line the walls of Louise's room today. Deanne, the couple's only daughter, is a respected cardiac nurse at

Roper Hospital. Finally, the middle son, Freddie, who built an entire car from scratch parts when he was in high school and later designed and built a hand glider he flew over Mt. Pleasant. He served as head of maintenance on the Yorktown carrier for years, working there while David did.

However, Freddie developed heart problems when he was in his mid-forties and needed a heart transplant. Eventually, he became too unwell to work. He was building a 'hot rod' from scratch when he passed away in December of 2014. The magazine *Garden and Gun* published an article on him in the February/March 2013 issue, The Shell Hunter.

"My children were all close, Deanne and Freddie. We're sad he's gone. My children meant everything to me. I figured if I had them, and if they wanted something, I'd get it for them. When Chevis, Jr., asked for that set of drums, but his daddy said no because he wanted him to learn classical music. So, I took a job as a school crossing guard making twenty-five dollar a week. I worked for months so I could buy Chevis those drums. It's kind of funny that it wasn't him who ended up playing drums after all, but David, and he still plays today."

Louise currently resides at Summit Place, and her room is full of the artistic talents and many accomplishments of her family from the over the years.

Pittsburgh, Pennsylvania - April 1928

Paul Richard Russell

Paul Russell was born in April of 1928 in a small town outside of Pittsburgh, Pennsylvania called Charleroi. Charleroi began as an industrial town that revolved around the manufacturing of glass. Like so many other communities in the North, the town was a melting pot of nationalities from across the Atlantic Ocean; people who had come to meet the demand for work during the Industrial Revolution. Among the immigrants, many were Belgians who brought their glass-making skills.

During the Industrial Revolution, the transition to new manufacturing processes in the period from 1760 to sometime between 1820 and 1840, Charleroi grew.

Eventually, it incorporated in 1891, during a time when glass was in a high demand nationwide. Just one year after The Charleroi Land Company applied for their charter of incorporation, the first glass plant in Charleroi was built. The Charleroi Plate Glass Company's plant was once one of the largest in the country. It's of no great surprise that Charleroi was named after Charleroi, Belgium, which at the time was the glass manufacturing capitol of the world.

Paul recalled his hometown to be about an hour's drive from Pittsburgh, yet geographically the towns are only twenty-one miles apart which is indicative of the slower transportation of his day. There, he attended public schools, enjoyed his education, and recalled his walks back and forth to school a couple of blocks away.

"There was no bus system for kids like now, so we simply walked to school, rain or shine."

It was actually in 1927 that the then Ford dealership owner, A.L. Luce, produced the first bus body for a Model T vehicle. Unlike previously built motorized buses with wooden bodies, Luce primarily used steel panels with wooden frames. This model would serve as the first bus design that would later be produced by the well-known bus manufacturer, Blue Bird. However, it wasn't until the years following World War II, when schools consolidated, relocated further apart from rural residents and the baby boom generation began their education, that school buses would become widely used.

Paul has one older sister by four years, Annetta. Their mother, Mina (short for Willamina), was a department store employee; the same store that would years later employ Paul part-time in high school for just twenty-five cents an hour as a stock boy. Their father, Placid Paul Russell, worked in a local glass-blowing plant during their childhood years, CorningWare Incorporated.

Corning was an American manufacturer of glass, ceramics, and related materials, primarily for industrial and scientific applications. The company was originally known as Corning Glass Works, until 1989 when it changed its name to Corning Incorporated. In 1998, Corning divested itself of its consumer lines, CorningWare, Corelle tableware and Pyrex cookware, and sold them to World Kitchen.

Unfortunately, Placid suffered a severe brain hemorrhage in January of 1940 when Paul was just twelve years old, and he passed away. Paul's sister, who was sixteen, and their mother, raised Paul from then on. Mina never remarried; she worked as the head cashier at Collins Department Store in Chareloi for most of her life to support her children. She lived a full life of ninety-seven years before she died.

In high school, Paul was in the marching band; he played bass clarinet for the football games and in-town parades in nearby Pittsburgh. Their family didn't own a vehicle, so had to get to the games by streetcar. Music played a big part of his life then and in the years to come. Once he finished high school, he went on to Dequesne University of the Holy Spirit, a private Catholic university in Pittsburgh, to study Music Education through the Mary Pappert School of Music.

The Pappert School of Music was founded in 1926 and offered a Bachelor of Music degree; the Music Education program was added in 1930. The school became accredited by the National Association of Schools of Music (NASM) in 1966; it became an 'all-Steinway' (Steinway is the most prominent of the concert piano companies known for making pianos of high quality) institution in 2001, and later an 'all-Fender' school (Fender is an American manufacturer of stringed instruments and amplifiers based out of Arizona).

While in college, Paul played the organ for numerous local events to earn money. One particular day, he recalled when he played the piano for a Catholic wedding for $15, a 'mixed' marriage for $10, a Jewish wedding for $15, and a Protestant wedding for $10. It all added up to a fair amount of cash for a young college student in those days.

He met a young lady around the time of his entrance into college, Mary. She was a year older and played the violin. Paul ended up being her sole accompanist in concerts, meaning whenever she would play, he played along with her. Without remorse and quite matter-of-factly, he recalled this about their nice yet relatively short-lived relationship:

> "We were pretty serious at the time; I even took her home to meet my mother and sister. We had a relationship for three years but broke up because she decided on someone else, some other guy who played the violin like her."

During college, Paul also worked at Kauffman's Department store selling men's shoes to help earn extra money. It was there that he met another girl, Rita, who was in nurses' training at a nearby school, the Mercy Hospital School of Nursing (MHSN), a 21-month, hospital-based diploma school of nursing, founded by the Sisters of Mercy in 1893. Today, MHSN is sponsored by UPMC Mercy, a part of the University of Pittsburgh Medical Center.

When they first met, Paul was in his last year of studies at Dequesne. Rita had come into the store to give a message to another associate. The message was from a girlfriend at the nurses' school who was sick and couldn't meet up with the guy there whom she was dating. Paul remembered this about that first introduction:

"I met Rita that day, but it wasn't until a week later before I found the nerve to give her a call. She did not play the violin, you see, or any other instrument, and that's what I knew.

"We eventually set up a date but without a car, we had to walk everywhere we went. So, I took her to some local, all-you-can-drink, bottomless cup coffee night cafe for our first date.

"Next, I think we went to some spaghetti place, then maybe a fast food joint. It didn't matter, we just had a great time together from day one. Though my mother had her heart set on me marrying my first girlfriend, she finally came around to liking Rita just as much as I did."

"Anyway, after college, I was away from Rita for three months for basic training before I was able to take a weekend and get back to Charleroi.

During the second trip home, my mother helped me select the ring I gave to Rita when I asked her to marry me. Rita's uncle was a Catholic Priest and he married us in the St. Paul cathedral in Pittsburgh in 1951." *

It was June of 1950 when Paul enlisted in the Air Force. He attended basic training at Sampson Air Force Base (AFB) in New York. His next assignment was at Craig AFB in Alabama, the same place where Martin Luther would begin his famous 50-mile walk to Montgomery on March 25th of 1965. King led thousands of nonviolent demonstrators to the steps of the capitol in Montgomery, Alabama after a five-day, 54-mile march from Selma, Alabama, where local African Americans, the Student Nonviolent Coordinating Committee (SNCC) and the Southern Christian Leadership Conference (SCLC) had campaigned for equal voting rights.

Paul's Air Force assignments took him from Craig Field, Alabama to Harlingen, Texas (Harlingen is the city with the least expensive cost of living in the United States and is also known for its mass production of citrus, primarily grapefruits). Despite his mother's limited financial means, she helped Paul buy a house trailer in Pennsylvania which he and Rita pulled from Charleroi to Alabama and then later to Texas for his next Air Force posting. After Texas, Paul was assigned to the Norton Air Force Base in San Bernardino, California.

One year later, Paul was sent to Bitburg, Germany where he served for three years at the American Spangdahlem Air Base. In December of 1944, Bitburg had been 85% destroyed by Allied bombing attacks and would later be officially designated by the U.S. military as a "dead city." Today, the most widely known Bitburg enterprise and landmark of the city is the Bitburg brewery; its Pilsener-style beer ranks number perhaps highest among Germany's best-selling breweries.

By this time spent in Germany, Paul and Rita would have three daughters, just twenty-two months apart: Patricia was the oldest, Mary was the middle girl, and Paula was the youngest. However, Paula was born with a defective hole in her heart. She was too young to have the heart surgery she needed as back then, that particular surgery was not performed until kids were nearly three years old.

With Rita unable to bring Paula to Germany at the start of Paul's stationing, for two of the three years he lived in Germany, his family stayed behind in San Bernadino. Paula's heart surgery was eventually performed at the Children's Hospital of Los Angeles, done by the same surgeon who performed the first open-heart surgery in Germany years before. Ater Paula successfully recovered, Rita and the girls followed Paul to Germany for the remainder of his assignment. He recalled this about their family time overseas:

> "We lived in the military housing section and had a German maid working for us, which of course my wife didn't mind. The area was the Mosel wine country, and we stayed up on a mountain, a twenty-mile drive down to Bittenburg each day. Mosel is one of thirteen German wine

regions known for quality wines. It takes its name from the Mosel River; before August of 2007, the region was known as Mosel-Saar-Ruwer.

"Then one weekend, we travelled in our little Volkswagen and went to the Alps for a tenting excursion. We were at the top of the Alps throwing snow at each other and it was the Fourth of July. Oh, and another family who was being re-stationed back in the States, they gave us this cat. He was a short-domestic grey I named, 'Herman the German' as our new family pet. When we left Germany, I sold the Volkswagen and took the cat to a farm nearby to find him a new home."

After Germany, Paul was assigned to Newport News, Virginia at Langley Air Force Base (AFB). He was there for seven years before he received his final overseas assignment in Korea at Osan AFB. He remained there for a thirteen-month assignment during which time he was unaccompanied by his family; only the base commander was allowed to bring his family.

There was no war during his time in Osan, as WWII had already ended, but Paul recalled how the Koreans did do a fair amount of stealing from the Americans. "One time, they disassembled an entire jeep, threw all of the parts over the fence one-by-one, and then reassembled it and drove away!" Some of the GI's moved into their girlfriend's local, apartments, and lived with them so they could save their housing allowance. Paul recalls eating lots of kimchi during his term in Osan, a traditional fermented Korean side dish made of vegetables with a variety of seasonings, often described as spicy and sour, and in traditional preparation kimchi is fermented underground in jars for months. It never quite made it to his favorite choice of dishes.

Because this was a relatively short assignment and due to distance, Paul did not come home midterm for the allowed thirty days. Instead, he taped a message to his wife and family with an old recorder and sent it to the States. By then, the couple's girls were ages eight, six and four. When Paul eventually left Osan, he was assigned to Charleston AFB; this is where he and their family would remain.

They first lived on-base in North Charleston, the year was 1962. Paul stayed in the Air Force for seven more years before retiring at the age fifty-five. He took a part-time job at Sears & Roebuck Co. then, working in their credit department, and soon left to accept a full-time job working for Robert Bosch. Paul was at Bosch for seventeen years as supervisor of the production department which assembled parts for the automobiles.

"I was the handler of supplies which I drew from the stock room to the floor. I remember Mrs. Fontenot's husband was also working there. I eventually retired from Bosch working in the Personnel department.

"One New Year's Eve, many were on vacation. I was driving to the plant about five miles away, when the battery in my car died. I had to walk the rest of the way, in a blizzard. They all looked at me like I was crazy, but I made it!"

During this time in Charleston, Rita returned to the working world as a registered nurse in Labor & Delivery at Roper St. Francis in West Ashley. Bon Secours Hospital can trace its mission back to 1882 when five Sisters of Charity of Our Lady of Mercy opened St. Francis Infirmary in downtown Charleston as the first Catholic hospital in the state. Rita worked until she retired to take care of her sister who was hospitalized for lung cancer due to smoking, until the day her sister passed away.

The couple's eldest daughter followed in her mother's footsteps and entered the healthcare profession. She still works at Roper St. Francis as a physical therapist. And day a week, Paul volunteers at the information desk in the Women and Children's Center. A smiling picture with his daughter and her son at the hospital is one of Paul's proudest family moments.

Rita and Paul enjoyed a retired life together for eight years before she became ill. She'd suffered from narrowing of the veins for many years and stayed in the hospital for only a month before she passed. Paul resides at Summit Place and refers to himself as a "Triple Dipper", as he is able to comfortably live off three pensions: the Air Force, Robert Bosch and Social Security. He has one sister remaining who lives in Charleroi, Pennsylvania with her daughter and family.

When asked about his life, Paul said, "If I could have done anything differently, I would have had a more varied life in the Air Force. More education there and going further in the service." What he is most proud of, is being married for fifty-four years, being healthy enough to work, and travelling the world with the Service to meet different people and enjoy unique and memorable experiences.

Saint Paul Cathedral is the 'mother church' of the Roman Catholic Diocese of Pittsburgh in Pennsylvania St. Paul's parish was established in 1834. When the diocese was established in 1843 St. Paul's Church was chosen as the cathedral.

Anderson County, Tennessee - August 1923

Wanda (Locket) Brown

Wanda Locket Brown was born in August of 1923 in Anderson County, Tennessee, land initially owned by the Eastern Band of Cherokee Indians. During Wanda's time, the town wasn't incorporated, but was rather "just a little place to live in the country… and very country", she said with a smile. When she was born, her father worked in the lumber business as did many men in the area, "cutting up the timber for selling." Anderson County is a mountainous region, though not very prosperous, and he made a living as best as he could for their family.

They lived very near a prison there, the Brushy Mountain State Penitentiary. Seemingly located in the 'middle of nowhere', the prison was built at the start of what is called the Devil's Triangle.

This is the most legendary motorcycle ride in the area, beginning near the prison on Hwy 116 and heading back to Oliver Springs. The scenic 72-mile route just north of Oak Ridge in the mountains of the Cumberland Plateau is made up of some of the most unusual, two-lane twisty roads in eastern Tennessee, and recommended for only the most experienced and adventurous riders.

In fact, Wanda's family lived so close to the prison, whenever there was a runaway inmate, they could hear the sirens notifying the town of the escape, along with the shrill barking of the bloodhounds used to track escapees down. It was a very secure site for a prison, though, and few inmates who escaped made it far.

Brushy Mountain Prison, which first opened its doors in 1896 and was known for its impressive architecture and for being a long-time family run business, housed some of the most dangerous criminals in Tennessee. The one, famous inmate sentenced to Brushy Mountain was one of the most despised felons of the twentieth century, James Earl Ray—the man who assassinated Reverend Martin Luther King, Jr. And he did try to escape with six other inmates in 1977 by climbing over the fence, but they were all captured two days later in the rugged mountain terrain, less than three miles away.

During their imprisonment time, Brushy Mountain convicts built a railroad spur, which is the track on which cars are left for loading and unloading and sometimes used for railroad car storage. The inmates also worked the coal mines and operated coke ovens.

A coke oven is a device used to produce coke, a product derived from coal; the mixing and heating of bituminous coal at temperatures ranging from around 1832° to 3632°F (1000° to 2,000°C) within an airless oven is what yields the coke byproduct. Some convicts farmed locally during their years of imprisonment.

Though the prison was eventually closed down in 2009, then Brushy was a looming presence in the background of Wanda's childhood. She had two sisters, one older by nine years and one younger by two years. They lived on a farm near Oliver Springs. Their father was Leeper Carter Locket, named after a pastor whom his parents had known and admired. Wanda said her father was very conscientious person and always taught them to do things right.

He used to say, 'You should never mistreat a child, cuz they'll never forget it.' And if we girls were doing something wrong, he would just turn and say to my mother,

'You'd better talk to them.' He never once laid a hand on us, but we never really gave him any trouble, either. If he said it, we did it." Their mother, Lily Jane Braden or "Lil", was a hard worker; Wanda remembered this about her:

> "Our daddy was gone a lot when he was in the logging business, even as far away as Kentucky, so our Mom did everything around the house. But we all had chores to do. There were farm animals, hogs, pigs and chickens, to take care of. But the cows were Mother's specialty.
>
> "She ran a home dairy and sold what she could. Every day, first thing, she'd take fresh milk, buttermilk, and butter down to Oliver Springs and deliver it all to her customers. Mom loved her cows and she loved to pick blackberries, too.
>
> "I heard the story where one season when she was pregnant with my baby sister and started to head out to pick berries, but my Aunt warned her that she'd have the baby in the field. My mother went anyway, so my aunt ran after her. My sister, the one in her belly, said she hated blackberries because of that, permanently marred by our mother's stubbornness."

In 1930, Anderson County and adjoining Campbell County started construction of the Norris Dam, a hydroelectric and flood control structure located on the Clinch River. Norris Dam was built as a storage dam, or a dam used to collect water and storage of water so it can be evenly distributed between locations. Because of the region's geography, mountains and valleys, flooding had been a significant problem to the people who lived there. For better pay that farming had provided them, Wanda's father took a job with the Tennessee Valley Authority (TVA) to help build the first dam.

Once he starting to work for the TVA, their family had no choice but to move around with the work as new dams in Tennessee and surrounding states were built. She said her family and other employers of the TVA became known as the "Dam Kids", and that's what they were called when they went into each new town and school.

The first move was to Savannah, Tennessee where the Pickwick Dam was built. The second move was to Guntersville, TN for the Guntersville Reservoir. Then, they moved to Murphy, North Carolina where the Hiawassee Dam was built, back to Tennessee for the Douglas Dam, then to Kingston, TN.

The family's final move was to Murphy, North Carolina where her father helped build the Chatuge Dam on the Hiwassee River. Murphy is where Wanda graduated from high school. After Wanda completed high school, around the war and the time of Pearl Harbor, her father was working on the Fontana Dam in Bryson City, North Carolina for the TNA.

The Tennessee Valley Association (TNA) operates the entire Tennessee River system and provides a wide range of public benefits, including year-round navigation, flood damage reduction, affordable electricity, improved water quality and water supply, recreation, and economic growth.

The organization established the stairway of these nine dams and locks, turning the Tennessee River into a 652-mile-long river highway, including storage dams and navigational dams.

All of these dams helped the land, economy and therefore the people of the region, all except for one. The Kingston Dam is known as one of the ten worst man-made environmental disasters in American history.

In December of 2008, the walls of the dam which held more than one billion gallons of coal ash, crumbled. A toxic concoction spilled into the town of Kingston; the wave of ash which was left over from burning coal mixed with water, wiped out roads, crumpled docks and destroyed homes. The ash was stored at the nearby Tennessee Valley Authority coal power plant and contained a decade's worth of arsenic, selenium, lead and radioactive materials.

The Kingston Dam spill was the largest industrial spill in U.S. history, and to this day the aftermath to the people who lived there is still unknown.

The year Wanda graduated from high school was 1940; half of her graduating class went into the army. Wanda wanted to get into some kind of defense work, as well, but her daddy said she had to go to school. At the time, women usually took Home Economics and attended college nearby, but that was not what Wanda wanted. Instead, she went to stay with her oldest sister who was by then married and lived in Clinton, Tennessee.

Wanda attended school at Draughons Practical Business College, a post-secondary education institution created in

1963 to help students achieve educational and career goals. Authorized by the Tennessee Higher Education Commission, it is now called the Daymar Institute and offers multiple locations in Tennessee. Wanda recalls this about her time spent in college, which was rather different than how things are done today:

> "You started taking courses and whenever you were ready, they would just send you out for a job. I had already taken most of the courses in high school, anyway. You had to have sixteen courses to graduate from high school and I had twenty-six, so it was fairly easy for me and I finished pretty quickly."

The first time they sent her on job, she learned of the requirement to have the smallpox vaccination, but the vaccine she was given as a baby hadn't taken. So, the company gave her another in her left arm which got infected and left a scar. Then the second one the doctor gave her in the knee also became infected. Wanda said she hadn't cared, because she was just happy to start a job. But when her parents came to visit, they saw her infections and said she had to come home. It wasn't long after, when a personnel officer from the TVA learned of Wanda's acquired and needed skills, and he asked her to work for them.

> "He repeatedly asked me to meet with them, but I kept telling him no. Then one day, I went to the grocery store for my mom and stopped by the TVA office without telling her. By the time I got home an hour later, they'd already sent me a

telegram from the home office saying I was hired.

The problem was, I had to move out of my parents' house because my daddy also worked at TVA and by company rules, we couldn't live in the same home. So, I moved in with a friend down the street, then went back-and-forth between her house and my childhood home. My infections eventually cleared up, and I loved my first 'real' job, I really did."

Soon after, the TVA sent Wanda to Fontana Dam, NC for her first assignment. She recalled the area as "the most God-forsaken country I had ever seen". She didn't want to stay, and thought if she simply didn't eat, she could get sick enough for her parents to have to take her back home again. However, the baker in the cafeteria at the dam facilities took a liking to her. He discovered her love for chocolate pies and cakes and baked enough for her to gain so much weight, she had no grounds for asking to return home.

Eventually, Wanda's father retired from TVA. He went back home to work on the farm in Oak Ridge. At the time, Oak Ridge was known as Clinton Engineering Works, a town conspicuously absent from any map of the United States. This 60,000 acres of farmland, framed by the foothills of the Appalachian Mountains, became one of the United States' three 'secret cities.'

The site was chosen by the Manhattan Project Director, General Leslie Groves. The Manhattan Project evacuated all Oak Ridge civilian inhabitants and built a plant for the specific purpose of producing an atomic bomb to be used against U.S. enemies during the war. The first atomic bomb built was called "Little Boy" and was dropped on Hiroshima, Japan in 1945. Wanda recalled this about those days:

"Suddenly, all of the farm lands were bought out, as the government came in and built the defense plant. Nobody really knew what they were doing. The government hired people to work there who didn't know what 'uranium' was. Guys drove around in government cars who walked through the town with maps under their arms, looking all serious and official.

"Farm owners would get a notice one day saying the government was taking over their property, and that was it. My sister and her husband were given two weeks' notice, then they had to find somewhere else to live."

"Farm animals were sold, hay was left in barns. Once people left, the dormitories, trailer parks, and flat top houses were secretly built for the plant. This all nearly happened overnight and created a ghost town."

Once Wanda's father left the TVA, she was allowed to live at home again. She tried to resign from the TVA and go, but they wouldn't release her from her duties at Fontanta Dam. Eventually, the division she worked with secured a government contract to manage the dormitories for the Manhattan Project, right back in Oak Ridge. They offered her a position there, then she gratefully returned to her hometown.

Oak Ridge was originally developed by the federal government as a segregated community. Black residents lived in the area known as Gamble Valley, and their assigned dwellings were government-built "hutments" or one-room shacks on the south side of town. With this history, and the mysterious government buildings, Oak Ridge became known a town of mystery. It now bears the following nicknames: *the Atomic City, the Secret City, the Ridge,* and *the City Behind the Fence.*

After the Manhattan Project closed down and the town of Oak Ridge was eventually incorporated, Wanda went to work as a city employee. She was there, making her own money and doing well for herself, when she met her future husband—by chance, when she wasn't looking. She'd been dating a guy from North Carolina at the time. Her neighbor was trying to fix her younger sister up with a boyfriend, so Wanda took her mother's buttermilk to the neighbor and brought her sister along.

> "I got into a discussion about football with the guy, who was supposed to be there for my sister. He and I argued about football and made a bet about who would win the next Alabama game. He asked me what we should bet on, and I replied, 'How 'bout a gallon of buttermilk against a watermelon.'
>
> "Well, I ended up winning the bet and he tracked me down to get me the watermelon I'd won.

However, melon season was about over, and you couldn't just buy them in the store back then. Together, we went out looking for one. We started dating then. I was twenty-six at the time, and in no hurry to get married, but Roy was persistent, I'll give him that much."

Wanda was married to Roy Giltz Brown for forty plus years before he passed away; she worked for the city of Oak Ridge for thirty-six years before retiring. The couple did not have children, though she considers her sisters' three children - a daughter by her oldest sister, and fraternal twins by her youngest sister - like her own "babies".

Wanda's youngest sister was stricken with arthritis at the age of thirty, so she couldn't play with or take care of her kids like Wanda could. Wanda has always behaved towards her children as if they were her own. Roy did, as well. Her sister passed away in 1998.

Wanda's other sister's girl twin, Marilyn, is a retired school teacher and lives near Wanda, in Charleston; Marilyn looks after Wanda "hand and foot" to help take care of her. Marilyn's mother, Wanda's older sister died from dementia in 1996, the same year her beloved Roy passed.

However, before Roy died, the couple had the opportunity to go on a wonderful trip together, to Switzerland. The year was in 1977, and though the trip was enjoyable, upon returning home Roy said he "never wanted to set foot on a plane again," and preferred to stay at home. From the trip, the travel bug bit Wanda, though, so when a friend asked her six years later to accompany her on a trip to Russia, she jumped at the chance.

Together, the women flew to Frankfurt, Germany and toured the Berlin Wall, then took a bus into Poland and finally to Russia. Her next trip with the same friend was to Egypt, then another to Greece, Ephesus (near Turkey, in the Bible), then to Argentina, and China, and Australia, New Zealand and Fiji.

She so enjoyed her time abroad. Wanda, a little ole country girl from Tennessee with the accent to prove it, became a world-traveler and enjoyed a wonderful life.

Swansea, South Carolina - August 1923

Katherine 'Kitty' (Asman) Proctor

Katherine 'Kitty' Proctor was born in 1923 just outside of Columbia, South Carolina in the small town of Swansea. As of 2010, the town's census had yet to reach a thousand residents. Her father, Neal Asman, was also born there, while Kitty's mother, Dolly was a 'mountain girl' from Asheville, North Carolina. Asheville is located at the confluence of the Swannanoa River and the French Broad River in the Blue Ridge Mountains. Today, the city enjoys various reputations including one of the 'happiest' places to live in the Southeast.

For Neal and Dolly, Kitty was one of eight children with two younger brothers, two older brothers and three sisters. A local African-American midwife, Adeline Porterfield, came to the Asman house to help deliver all of Dolly's children through the years.

> "There was about fifteen months between each of us, which was pretty impressive considering we all lived in a two-bedroom home (she said this with a grin). My daddy slept with all the boys in one room, while my momma slept with the girls in the other. It was crowded, for sure, but we didn't know any better back then and life was good."

During her formative years, Kitty and her siblings were all strictly reared. Their father watched over everything and ruled with an 'iron fist' when he wasn't working in the fields. Kitty's mornings were spent at school with her siblings. They had to walk five miles together to get there as schools didn't yet offer transportation system, nor did they serve lunch. Students who lived in the country arrived home around two in the afternoon, ate their lunches, then immediately started on their farm chores. With a household of ten, chores were a necessary part of all of the Asman children's lives.

They did not participate in after-school or extra-curricular activities. But, Kitty said, kids got plenty of exercise in those days, and today they don't. "Kids should be out in the yard and working alongside their parents, instead of everyone hiring people to do everything. Parents just let them sit around playing games all day. It's not good for them." When asked about her own childhood days, Kitty laughed and said this:

"Somehow, we always found something to play with and entertain us, even though we never really had toys, not like kids do nowadays. We had plenty of food, too. It might not have been what we wanted, but when momma put food on the table, you ate it.

"My momma, she baked bread a lot. She was a good cook, but she was just a wonderful baker and it always made our house smell so good.

"We wore hand-me-down clothes, too, because it's all we had. I remember I had this brown coat someone gave me, and a boy in school used to call me 'Brown Coat Girl,' to make fun. Oh, I hated that coat so much."

Without a house large enough to accommodate all eight children, the outdoors served as the Asman children's playground. During the hot summers, there were ponds near their house to cool off, yet only the boys learned how to swim. The girls knew not to go in too deep, and even as an adult, Kitty never learned how to swim.

The closest beach was only about an hour and forty-five minutes away from Swansea, yet they never made it to the ocean. "The first time I saw Folly Beach, I almost died, it was so beautiful," Kitty recalled.

Her father worked as a tenant farmer, a person who farms the land of another and pays rent with cash or with a portion of the produce from the land. Though he grew vegetables such as tomatoes and corn, cotton was his main crop. Cotton planting season begins as early as February in southern Texas and extends as late as June in the northern areas of the Cotton Belt, which extends up to Maryland.

Currently, cotton is being grown in seventeen states and one bale of cotton can make 1,217 men's T-shirts or 313,600 one-hundred dollar bills. However, China is the world's leading producer of cotton at approximately thirty-three million bales per year, with India being second at twenty-seven bales; the United States follows up third with an average of seventeen million bales of cotton every year. Kitty recalled this about those farming days:

> "Together with the hired hands, we kids helped plant the cotton seed each year. It comes in

burrs, and back then you had to go through it all and pick it by hand. Some of the black women, they had could pick a hundred pounds in a day and I was always so mad that I couldn't do that.

"The weight was what determined how much they made, and at the end of the day, they would tie up their pickings and weigh them with my daddy. This one day, a woman's bag was too much weight, and when my daddy opened it up, he saw the girl had put three bricks in there to make it heavier. I don't know for sure, but I'm guessing she didn't stay with us after that."

She graduated from high school at the age of seventeen. From there, she went to work at the then-famous S.H. Kress, in nearby Columbia. At the time, S.H. Kress & Co., which was open from 1896–1981, was one of the twentieth century's most prosperous variety-store retailers. Though it was never the largest chain, from 1927 Kress maintained the highest per-store sales of any five-and-dime retailer up and did so until about 1947.

The creation of an architectural division within the company is what played a key role in attracting customers and facilitating sales. The company's founder, Samuel H. Kress (1863–1955), had envisioned his stores in the communities as works of public art that would contribute to the cityscapes.

To distinguish his stores from competitors, namely F.W. Woolworth Co. at the time, he hired staff architects to design his buildings. Kress achieved retail branding success not merely through standardized signage and graphics, but through distinctive architecture and an efficient design for each store. From elaborate Gothic Revival to streamlined Art Deco designs, Kress stores were built to be integral parts of their business districts and helped define Main Street America in the day.

As for Kitty, she was eventually promoted to the information desk with Kress, before then moving on to work at Citizens and Southern (C & S) National Bank as a bookkeeper and later as a teller. After a subsequent merger with NCSB to form Nations Bank, C & S bank was bought by Bank of America.

The former Charleston C & S location, Citizens and Southern National Bank of South Carolina, is the second oldest bank building in the U.S. and possibly the oldest still used as a bank. Constructed in 1798 as the Bank of South Carolina, it later became the home for the Charleston Library Society (1835), belonged to the Charleston Chamber of Commerce (1914), and finally became a bank again when C & S purchased the two-story building in 1966. Still located at 50 Broad Street, the building now serves as a private office building.

C & S Bank was also significant because it's where Kitty met her husband. Thomas Orr Proctor had been visiting the bank for his own work at the ice plant. He winked at Kitty when he saw her, then he went back to tell her manager, "I want what that teller out there has in her drawers!" He was cheekily referring to her bank deposit drawers, of course, but his comment spurred their first date.

They were later married in 1945 in Casey, West Columbia, at a cousin's house; "I just wore a navy-blue suit I had; I couldn't afford to buy anything new. One of my sisters did the reception after, with sandwiches and lemonade, but no alcohol."

Before Kitty and Thomas had married or even met, he served as a Navigator Cadet in the Army Air Force and in Germany. And by the time their paths crossed, Thomas was known locally as the "Ice Man" because he was the manager for the ice plant in town. Ice plants were used before "automatic refrigeration" as fridges were originally known, came into production. When the business ended, Thomas then took a sales job traveling for McCormick and Council, the spice company, until one day he had a debilitating traffic accident and could no longer travel or work.

After Thomas' accident, he decided to open up a local restaurant in Charleston called the Okay Diner. At some point, Kitty decided she'd enough of banking and left her job to help him run it. She quickly changed the name to Kitty's Diner, and they rented their building for ten years before eventually buying it outright. She changed the name again, to Kitty's Fine Foods, and her restaurant became well-known in Charleston for serving Southern food. *

She never served alcohol there, though, as that was the manager's one request when she rented the building, and Kitty didn't see a need to change it. Kitty's Find Foods served old-style soul food such as black-eyed peas and collard greens, and the restaurant fed up to seventy people for breakfast and lunch each day, closing before dinner. Altogether, she worked in, managed or owned the restaurant for twenty-seven years. She said this about her time there:

> "It wasn't a job for me, because it was so much fun. I was there first thing in the morning when we opened for breakfast, 6a.m. And I stayed through the lunch rush until 3p.m nearly every day.
>
> "My customers and the gals who worked for me made everything great. I never had to worry about anyone taking from me and together, we served some of the finest people— the cream of the crop, I would say—in Charleston. I saw everyone at our tables, from the Mayor and the Governor to the street sweepers. We served them all."

When Thomas had worked at the ice plant and Kitty was still at the bank, they lived in an apartment in West Ashley for ninety dollars a month. One day, a man walked into the bank and told Kitty he had a small apartment for rent for just thirty-five dollars a month, out on Sullivan's Island. Sullivan's Island had served the point of entry for approximately forty percent of the 400,000 enslaved Africans who were brought to British North America.

The island has been likened to Ellis Island, the 19th-century reception point for immigrants in New York City. During the American Revolution, Sullivan's island was the site of a major battle at Fort Sullivan on June 28, 1776 and was renamed Fort Moultrie in honor of the American commander at the battle. Today, Sullivan's island is a beautiful island that attracts beach-lovers from all around, and several districts and properties on Sullivan's Island have been listed in the National Register of Historic Places.

For Kitty and Thomas, Sullivan's Island is where the couple's son, Thomas Jr., was born. The couple built their family home that same year, in 1949, for thirteen thousand dollars. When they moved in, Kitty said she felt so lucky to be there. And they had a wonderful neighbor who lived next door whom their son Thomas called 'Aunt Ruth' because the woman helped take care of him when Kitty worked the restaurant.

The Proctor house is located near the Sand Dunes Club, and with the renovations their son has since made to the home and tis ideal location, the home's value has increased beyond expectation. Thomas, Jr. still lives in their family home, now with his own wife and children. Kitty, a resident at Summit Place on Daniel Island, feels she led a good life without regret for a anything. The newspaper articles about her accolades with the restaurant line her bedroom walls are proof.

At the time of print, the restaurant location is currently being occupied by the Tattooed Moose at 1137 Morrissey Drive in Charleston.

Lonsdale, Tennessee - December 1932

Betty (Martin) Rollings

Betty Martin was born in the small community of Lonsdale in Knoxville, Tennessee, to Dora Lee and Harry William Martin. When she was four years old, Betty's parents chose to separate after ten years of marriage together. Her father moved to Macon, Georgia and lived first with his mother, then later with another woman for eighteen years before he passed away. In all those years, he returned home just once to see his family.

Betty, two of her three siblings and their mother, moved in with her Dora Lee's parents, William Arthur Turner and

Cathryn "Cate" Viola Turner. They lived just a block down the street and quickly became the foundation of Betty's childhood. About this early period of her life, and in particular her parent's separation, Betty had this to say:

> "Mother never said a negative word about my daddy after he left, even though when he went to Georgia, he took my older brother, Charles, with him. Charles was just five years old at the time. We also had an older sister who was eight years old, and daddy wanted to take her, too, but our mother refused to let her go because she was old enough to go to the store and help her out around the house.
>
> "Then two years after daddy moved out, mother left for Macon one day with some of her friends. She desperately wanted to try to get her son back. I know she was able to talk to Charles there, but I don't believe the thought ever occurred to her to just take Charles and leave, and our father refused to let him go.
>
> "Momma left Macon without Charles, and that was the last time she got to see her son until he was eighteen years old. By then, none of the family even knew Charles and, sadly, he was never a part of our lives. Growing up, I was close with my other brothers and sisters, but after we all moved away, things changed between us all."

The one time that Betty's father ever came to see Dora Lee, Betty was by then nineteen, married and pregnant with her first child. She recalled sitting at the kitchen table and seeing her father for mere minutes. He never talked directly to her, then left the house soon after.

Two years later, when her first son was eighteen months old, Betty took him to see 'Grandma Martin,' her father's mother, down in Georgia. Her father was still living in the home with his mother and though the visit was pleasant, he only returned to the house after they had all gone to bed, then snuck out the next morning before anyone awoke.

Growing up, it was her mother and her mother's parents Betty remembers with fondness. The women did all the family cooking on an old, coal stove in the kitchen and served three hot meals a day, including pies, biscuits and breads. For dinner, they had staple meals such as liver and onions, or ham dinners. Their mother never made the kids eat anything they didn't like, but if there were complaints, she wouldn't cook anything else.

There was a grocery store close by where her mother did the daily shopping, and Betty's grandfather would walk over and pay their grocery bill every Friday. Betty said she can still see in her mind how he much enjoyed his daughter's cooking in the evening after work. Her grandfather would finish off his plate until it was clean, and take the bone from the ham, cut off the ends, and then suck all of the marrow from the middle. She pictured him sitting in a kitchen chair backward and watching over her and her younger sister playing at his feet.

Interestingly, though her grandfather never talked about the time he spent in the war, he had served in the 1898

Spanish-American War, a conflict between Spain and the United States as a result of the United States' intervention in the Cuban War of Independence. Betty said her grandfather was caring, kind, and good to his grandchildren. He worked hard to support their family, and they had a good life because of him. Even though there were never extras, Betty and her siblings always had enough food on the table and clothes on their backs.

Her grandfather worked for years at Miller's Department Store as a watchman on weekends and packing items to be shipped from the store during the week. Miller's Store first opened its doors in New York City in 1859. A son of Gus Miller became one of the founders of Miller, Inc., down in Knoxville, Tennessee. Then in 1981, with the acquisition of its parent conglomerate, Miller's became a part of Allied Stores, and in 1990, it was converted to a Dillard's.

"I didn't know I had a bad childhood from my father leaving us because my grandparents were so good to me. We really were quite happy together during my growing up years."

Betty attended Rule High School, a public high school in Knoxville, Tennessee that opened its door to students in 1927 though eventually closed in 1991. The school was named after Knoxville newspaper editor Captain William Rule (1839–1928). In 1937, an effort was made to append a grade twelve to the school curriculum. However, the appeal initially fell through and on April 14, 1937, six hundred students from grades seventh through eleventh who wanted twelfth grade, staged a walkout protest. The protest was reported on the front page of the New York Times; and paved the way for subsequent classes, including Betty's, to complete their schooling there.

Betty played basketball through the local 'Y' and softball through their church. She was at a church event one night when she met the man who would become her husband. They were attending a class, and he had come from one of five other churches in the Knoxville area. All the young adults were divided by age into different rooms and as he was eighteen years old and she had just turned 17, they were in the same classroom.

During the lesson, the teacher commented on the dangers of smoking, something he vocally agreed to, as Betty recalled. Yet when the meeting was over and they all left the church, she was flabbergasted to see that same young man pull out a pack of cigarettes outside and light up.

Before she could stop herself, she said something cheeky to him about his arrogant and rather hypocritical words in the meeting. Her comment sparked his interest, and the next night after class Howard Louis Rollings didn't go home with his parents but instead asked Betty if he could walk with her.

"Howard, he was stubborn. He didn't tell me he loved me for four months after we met. His friend Jimmy started dating my friend Betty around the same time, and Jimmy told Betty he loved her on their second date. But Howard and I did marry next February.

"I was finishing my junior year, and Howard went into the service the following August. In the middle of my senior year, I left to follow him to Fort Devins near Ayer, just outside of Boston, Massachusetts. Then the following summer, I came back home to attend summer school and got my high school diploma."

Howard entered the service with ten-thousand other National Guards during the Korean War (1950 - 1953). The National Guard is part of the reserve components of the U.S. Armed Forces, and their units are under dual control of the state and the federal government. They are also members of the militia of the U.S., due to the group's origin.

Local militia were formed from the earliest English colonization of the Americas dating back to the early 1600's, and the title "National Guard" was used around 1825 by some New York State militia units, named after the French National Guard in honor of the Marquis de

Lafayette. The name 'National Guard' became a standard nationwide militia title in 1903. Though many National Guard forces were sent to Iceland and some to Korea during the war, as a cook for the army, Howard was never re-stationed outside the U.S. He served the full, two years in Massachusetts.

Three years after they were married, Betty and Howard welcomed their first child, Steven Mark. Two years later, they had a daughter they named, Teri, then a second son, Louis "Matt" Matthew was born four years later.

After Howard left the service, he took a job driving a truck selling tobacco products to local businesses. He drove a truck for a year before he went to work in the by-then famous 'Oak Ridge' facility in Tennessee. There, he worked for 'Carbide', or the Union Carbide & Carbon Corporation, at the K-25 plant in Oak Ridge - a former uranium enrichment facility of the top-secret government endeavor, the Manhattan Project.

The code name 'K-25' for the plant was a combination of the "K" from the Kellex Corporation, who were the initial contractors of the plant, and '25' which was the World War II-era code designation for uranium-235. Gaseous diffusion was the primary method for processing in the development of nuclear weapons. It was one of three isotope separation processes that provided uranium-235 for the Hiroshima nuclear weapon nicknamed "Little Boy".

During the 1950s-1960s, Union Carbide used mercury for the separation of another component of nuclear weapons, lithium-6. Though 1/3 of the world's mercury was brought in to Oak Ridge during those years, some 2.4 million pounds of mercury are still unaccounted for today. While much of it is likely buried underneath the destroyed buildings of the Oak Ridge complex, it is known that up to 475,000 pounds of mercury leaked into the creek, and 30,000 pounds are believed to have been leaked into the air. In 1955, nearly half of workers tested had mercury in their urine at levels above those considered to be safe.

After the Korean War ended, and the Carbide plant's production was no longer needed, the government laid off nearly 10,000 workers in Oak Ridge, including Howard. This layoff occurred two months short of his ten-year retirement to receive a pension, so Howard never received another penny for his employment.

For many years, Oak Ridge's remote location in Tennessee and low population helped keep the town and its nuclear military creations a secret from the rest of the world. Even as the population of the settlement grew from 3,000 to 75,000 from 1942-1945, the place was kept 'under wraps.' Interestingly, it was the national news release of the use of the first atomic bomb against Japan on August 6, 1945, that finally revealed its location. And to the people who had been employed and living at Oak Ridge, may finally discovered just what they had worked on. Today, the area still has a few of the buildings left over from the Project, including a standing Chapel built for the workers, yet mostly it's become a site of historic fascination. Betty had this to say this about her husband's employment:

> "I always thought Howard was testing something, but I wasn't sure. What I remember

most is that he usually worked the swing shift, so it was tough to keep the kids quiet during the day while he slept. I never knew much about the place, other than it paid the bills."

After Oak Ridge laid off Howard, he first took a job selling and delivering milk. "Here's a cute story," she said with a twinkle in her eye. "He was *our* neighborhood milkman, and I would leave notes for him with our empty bottles on our porch. He'd pick up my little notes and carry them around all day."

However, as Howard made half of what he'd made at K-25, he soon left and went to work for a finance company for the higher pay. Betty said, although she and her husband had always planned to have four children, they stayed with three due to their financial situation.

During those early married years, Betty Rollin's love for children did not stop within the home. She had it in her heart to be a teacher, so after her youngest child turned five and started elementary school, Betty went to college. She enrolled at East Tennessee State University; at thirty-six years old, she was one of the oldest graduates in the program. It took her five years to complete her first degree.

She soon started teaching at local schools, and eventually went on to earn her Master's in Elementary Principalship. She taught first grade one year, third grade another, and second grade for the rest. Betty taught for twenty-six years before retiring from the school system.

Though out of the school system for some years now, she said teaching had already begun to change; a long, gradual change that reflected society, parenting and the times. She recalled this about a teaching moment:

> "One day, we had a mother come into the school, it was just before I retired. She was very upset about something and actually attacked a teacher. You would never have seen such behavior when I first started teaching, but things had already changed. I can't imagine what teachers have to deal with today."

As for Howard, through the finance company he worked for, he was eventually transferred to Kingsport, Tennessee. He worked there for three plus years before he took a job at the First Tennessee bank in Johnson City. Howard stayed with this bank for twenty-six years and retired as Branch Manager. However, the smoking habit that first brought he and Betty together was his demise, for after smoking for most of his life, he suffered one heart attack and then another twelve years after.

> "Losing Howard was very difficult, and my mother died five months after. She'd been living in a nursing home in Rutledge, Tennessee. Howard and I had already talked about bringing her home with me before he died. Our Doctor said he would take her on as a patient if I brought mother home to Johnson City, but she died before we could bring her home.
>
> When my mother passed away at the nursing home, my son Matt was there with her. I missed seeing her by just four minutes. I held her anyway,

because people say folks can still hear after you stop breathing, even just for a bit. I held onto her and told her I loved her, over and over."

After her husband and mother passed away, Betty spent the next year and a half of her life packing up and taking care of things. She bought a small house in Shadowmoss Plantation, West Ashley, one she still owns and rents to one of her granddaughters today.

"Back then, there were 1900 homes in the Shadowmoss Plantation and many were right on the golf course. The development had lakes everywhere for aesthetics. It was a delightful place to live, but I missed Howard and my mother.

"Though right out of high school, Howard was a wonderful husband and made a decent living for us. We had a good marriage, and I loved every minute of being a wife and a mother."

Of her family, Betty's two brothers are both deceased, but her sisters both live in Knoxville. One sister, Peggy, is a widow and still lives in her own home; her children don't live nearby, but her grown grandchildren do, and they help take care of her. The other sister, Wanda is still married to husband, Jim. Betty's grandmother who'd helped raise her, died young at the age of 56 when Betty was just fourteen. Her 'Grandpa' lived to be seventy and he passed away months after Betty's son Mark was born.

Today, Betty's son Mark and his wife Karen live in Wintersport, Maine. Teri, Betty's daughter, is a civil engineer and lives in Winona, Delaware, along with her two daughters who live nearby. Betty's youngest son, Matt, and his wife Sandy live in Charleston; they also have two grown daughters nearby. Betty resides at Summit Place and feels blessed to have had such a wonderful life.

"Looking back, I can't think of a single regret. I was poor but didn't know it. We went to church, praised God, and sang in the youth choir. My children were baptized and saved. Reverend J. Birch Cooper and Ed McCollum were our pastors. I taught Sunday School. My grandparents were good people and I had it good."

Birmingham, Alabama - August 1923-July 2015

Lucille (Starnes) O'Connell

Lucille Hilton Starnes was born in St. Vincent's Hospital in Birmingham, Alabama in August of 1923. Her mother, Lucille Gorden Hilton, was raised there, as well. The pace of Birmingham's growth from 1881 through 1920 earned the city such nicknames as *The Magic City* and *The Pittsburgh of the South*.

Much like Pittsburgh, Birmingham's major industries were iron and steel production, plus a major component of the railroading industry, as both rails and railroad cars were manufactured there. During the civil rights movement of the 50's and 60's, Dr. Martin Luther King wrote the now famous "Letter from Birmingham Jail" while imprisoned for participating in a nonviolent protest there - the letter was a defining treatise in his cause against segregation.

Lucille's mother was the oldest of six sisters, and all but one of those sisters remained in Birmingham into their adulthood. However, Lucille's mother experienced such a difficult pregnancy Lucille was their only child. Her mother didn't work outside of the home. For most of Lucille's childhood the family had hired help around the house who were like part of the family.

They employed one woman named Azula for almost ten years; she didn't live with them, but came to the house every day to cook, clean and help take care of Lucille. Azula was the one who picked Lucille up from school at Norwood Elementary every day and did most everything for her. When asked what her mother did while Lucille was at school, Lucille's response was this. "I don't know, maybe play bridge. Really, I'm just not sure."

Neither of her parents had come from any significant amount of family money. Her father, Thomas Montgomery Starnes, grew up on a farm in North Carolina and had to end his schooling in the eighth grade to go to work and help his family. He worked hard and eventually became a sales manager for ACIPCO (the American Cast Iron Pipe Company); he travelled all over the Southern States for them. Today, ACIPCO is the world's largest, single-site manufacturer of ductile iron pipe, fire hydrants, and valves for water works applications, electric resistant steel pipe for oil and natural gas pipelines.

While in middle and high school, Lucille was well-liked, popular and active. She played kickball, tennis and golf, yet her real love was always for dancing. Lucille started taking lessons at the age of four—ballet, tap and jazz. She continued only with ballet and took lessons through high school. She danced professionally for the then distinguished Saxon Dance Studio in Birmingham until she graduated from high school.

After high school, Lucille attended Ward-Belmont College in Nashville, Tennessee and studied dance for two years. Ward Seminary and Belmont College for Young Women had merged in 1913 to form Ward-Belmont, and it was the first junior college in the South to receive full accreditation by the Southern Association of Colleges and Secondary Schools. By the 1920s, it had an enrollment of more than 1,200 women.

Ward was a women's college, also known at the time as "ladies' seminary school", located on the grounds of an old antebellum estate. Regarded as a very prestigious finishing school by the more aristocratic families of Middle Tennessee, such names as Minnie Pearl (given name, Sarah

Colley Cannon), Mary Martin (who played Maria von Trapp in the Broadway production of *The Sound of Music*), and Amy Grant attended the school.

After two years, Lucille then went on to the University of Texas and earned her Bachelor of Fine Arts in Dance. Although the University of Texas has a notable drama program, she also chose the school because a number of her friends were going there. She successfully completed her schooling in dance, despite having sustained a hip injury during high school, and then headed to New York City to pursue her career. Given the era, and as a lone woman, it is quite impressive that Lucille went to the 'big city' to follow her dreams.

At the time, there were places in NYC where women could live temporarily and safely; apartments with chaperones and supervisors who would watch over the girls. Lucille stayed at the well-known Three Arts Club while she was in New York. Back in 1909, right after the Three Arts Club had opened, the establishment was described as such: "Its history is the narrative of a struggle for the fundamental uplifting of the stage, by supplying its novitiates a suitable home at reasonable rates during the trying weeks and months which precede the first happy hours of real achievement as an artist." In sum, it was a place to stay for newcomers and rising stars who could soon make it big.

While in NYC, Lucille tried out for the famous Rockettes Dance Group, a precision dance company known for a style of dance, a mixture of both modern dance and classic ballet. The company was founded in St. Louis,

Missouri in 1925, but the Rockettes moved to the Radio City Music Hall in Manhattan, NYC in 1932 - fifteen years before Lucille auditioned.

After nearly one hundred years, the Rockettes still perform five shows a day, seven days a week for the public during the Christmas season. Their best-known routine is an eye-high leg kick done in perfect unison in a chorus line at the end of every performance. Auditions are in April and women must show proficiency in several genres of dancing, mainly ballet, tap, modern, and jazz.

Normally, four hundred to five hundred women audition yearly, and every Rockette must be between 5'6" and 5'10½" tall. The illusion that all Rockettes are the same height is created by placing the tallest women at the center of the line and then in descending height order to the ends. Performing a 'personality kick' (when toes are eye level) ensures all the kicks will appear to be at exactly the same level with no one dancer kicking higher than any other. As for Lucille, although she was chosen, she was not pleased about the details of her acceptance and said this about the opportunity.

> "Because I was just 5'6" tall, I would have been placed at the very end of the dance line and that wasn't good enough. So, after being away for two years, I decided I was homesick enough. I left New York and went back to Alabama."

She'd dated a boys in college and some in New York City; one man in particular man was Bob June. In World War II, he'd named his fighter plane after Lucille, "Lulu".

But it wasn't until she moved back to Birmingham when she met her future husband, Richard Merritt O'Connell. She knew of Richard while in high school, as she attended Phillips High School and he attended the nearby Ramsey High. It was after he'd returned home from the war, stationed in Germany and then France with the Army, when they met.

> "He had bad eye sight, yet desperately wanted to jump out of planes as a paratrooper, so he memorized the eye chart to try to pass the exam, but the doctors discovered his trick and stuck him on the ground in the Army, instead."

Richard had one brother and a half-sister, Lute. Their mother was born into a well-to-do family in Montgomery, Alabama; Kathleen O'Connell O'Connell (Lucille's father, Edward O'Connell, was her second husband, which is why her name included O'Connell twice.) It was Lute's father who came one day and swept Kathleen off her feet. He whisked her away to New Orleans to get married, and soon she was pregnant with Lute. However, few years after, she somehow managed to get the marriage annulled because apparently, he was a bit of a scoundrel. She later married Richard's father.

Lucille was teaching third grade at Norwood Elementary, the school she attended twenty years before. One day, Richard came to Lucille's home to pay her a visit and brought his best friend, Jimmy Chenoweth, for support. Lucille and Richard started dating soon after; for two years they played tennis, went to the movies, and enjoyed the theater, before eventually marrying.

"Richard was as handsome as anyone and a well-known ladies' man. His nickname in college was "Tricky Dicky the Campus Quickie."

There was a significant obstacle to their marriage, however, for Richard's family was Catholic and Lucille's family was Methodist – a bigger deal in 1945. Neither of their parents wanted them to marry outside of their religion, so the couple switched to Episcopalian and became members of the local Episcopalian Church, instead.

Because they didn't think their families would support their union nor wouldn't attend the wedding, Lucille chose a simple green dress with a small hat, instead of the typical flowing white wedding gown. However, one-by-one, family from both sides starting pouring into the church. It was a grand and wonderful wedding for them both. Jimmy, Richard's best friend, went with Richard and Lucille on their honeymoon in Daytona Beach, Florida, and would remain a lifelong friend to them both.

Three years later, they had their first daughter and named her Lucille, though she was called Cile to differentiate from her mother and her grandmother before her. Two plus years after, they had their second daughter and named her Shali, after Lucille's favorite perfume (Guerlain Shalimar) and the little town in Florida located in Okaloosa County where the couple often travelled to.

Richard had attended the University of Virginia for two years after high school, before being drafted into war. He'd been studying to become a psychiatrist, but when he returned from the war his father discouraged him from pursuing such an "unstable" profession, for something more grounded. Richard finished his remaining two years at the University of Alabama (UA), then went on to get his Master's in Business.

During Richard's studies in graduate school, Lucille worked in the local women's department store to help support them. They also owned a paper route, and every morning before dawn, one would drive and the other would throw the newspapers out the window. Richard accepted a job with Southern Bell after completing his schooling.

Lucille accompanied him on his interview. When the interviewer asked Richard if he could perform some specific task and he replied "yes", Lucille piped up and loudly exclaimed, "No, you cannot!". He was still offered the job, and Richard was transferred to Tuscaloosa with Southern Bell, the first of many moves, about every three years. And just as Lucille had while growing up, she hired a helper to take care of the girls after Shali was born, one who had worked for Lucille's mother. Her name was Jessie Jefferson and became part of the family:

> "She was a very large black woman who always wore a bandana on her head. She was big and imposing, but very sweet and once Shali was born, Jessie took right to my daughter and loved her like her own.
>
> "When we moved to Tuscaloosa for Richard's work, she moved with us. Jessie stayed with our family, helping with the girls and doing the cooking and cleaning, until we returned to Birmingham when Richard was transferred back. She then went back to work for my mother until the day she retired."

The O'Connell family then moved to Atlanta, back to Birmingham, and finally to Anchorage, Kentucky, a small town outside of Louisville. By this time, Cile was in the fourth grade and Shali was in first, and Richard and Lucille decided they would be there to stay. They sold their house in Birmingham and settled down for the remainder of the girls' childhood. (Besides a one and half year stint in Connecticut while the girls were in middle/high school, when Richard worked in NYC, commuting four hours a day so his family could live in a nicer area.)

The family had horse stables growing up in Kentucky and about four acres of land. After school, the kids would ride their backyard ponies until dark. Lucille was actively involved in her daughters' lives. She served as a Brownie and Girl Scout leader for years. She taught Cile field hockey which Cile would later play in college and even taught Physical Education for one year at their school, after the school's coach suffered a heart attack.

Yet perhaps most importantly, Lucille turned their basement into a full-fledged dance studio so her girls could dance. For many years, Lucille taught the local girls the ballet moves she'd so loved as a child. Even when her hip injury became too much to allow her to teach, Lucille's passion for the arts did not stop.

Then, she spearheaded the creation of the Anchorage Cookbook through their church, and hand wrote every recipe in the book for it to be published. Her talents extended to painting, as well, and later in life she painted dozens of watercolor works—of personal portraits, people's homes and churches, a few of which hang in her room and in friends' home around the South.

She also tried her hand at the theatre and directed a play called 'The Apple Tree', a series of three musical playlets, each one has its own storyline, and all three were tied together by a common theme. The play was performed at the Mummers and Minstrels, an Anchorage community theater group that has performed one big show a year since 1958. Back then, they used to create original musicals and perform them in the backyard of the company's creator, Mavis McGhee. As for Lucille's play, it was a huge success. She wouldn't accept money for her work on it and was given a dozen apple trees as a gift, instead. Her family planted the trees in a line in front of their home.

After Cile and Shali left home to start their own lives, Richard opened up a retail store in town called The Sporting Life. Lucille worked with him, and together they began selling tennis clothes because there were no women's tennis dresses for sale in town at the time (Cile had to play on the boys' tennis team back in high school). They later brought in golf clothes and eventually regular wear for women. Lucille mainly ran the business while her husband worked at the phone company. She did all the ads for the store and Richard came up with the catchy phrases to go along with them.

After they sold the store, the couple moved to Jacksonville, Florida and opened up a new location there. They named it, The Sporting Life Limited. After they sold the store, the couple officially retired, but Richard had another grand idea and opened a new store. This time, they carried all French items, and he called the store the French Country Store de Provence. It was located in Ponte Vedra Beach, near Jacksonville in a very well-to-do resort area. Sales did not go as well as expected, though, so they sold the store after three years and finally stopped working to enjoy their retirement.

From ballet to the Rockettes, from cookbooks to plays, Lucille led a rich, fulfilling life and shared wonderful memories with family and friends. Sadly, her husband passed away on their 61st wedding anniversary. Although she missed him dearly, Lucille looked back on her accomplishments, as a dancer, a painter, volunteer, wife and mother with well-deserved love and pride. Lucille herself recently passed while living at Summit Place, leaving their two loving daughters behind. Her sweet spirit and warm smile will be missed by all.

Detroit, Michigan - June 1935

James "Jim" Sexauer

James "Jim" Sexauer was born in Detroit, Michigan in June 1935. His father, Frederick William Sexauer, was born in Lancaster, Ohio along with one brother. But Jim's mother, Lorna Gunther, was Canadian by birth and the last of eleven children in her family, from a small town in Ontario, Canada.

Her parents decided to move to Detroit, Michigan when Lorna was seven years old, along with the siblings still living at home. Upon hearing her accent in Detroit, people often didn't believe that Lorna was American and would tease her. When they asked her to recite the English alphabet to prove she was, she quickly learned to say "A, B... and Z", instead of "A, B... and Zed", as many non-nationals and Europeans will do.

Jim's father, Frederick, was a serious and determined man who ruled their house with a heavy hand. He'd been married to another woman before he married Jim's mother, and he had a child in his first marriage, Freddie. A year after Freddie's mother passed away, Frederick met and then married Lorna. Frederick and Lorna had one daughter together, Lorna Lou, then two years later they had Jim and finally son, Charles Paul, born in 1942.

Growing up, his father had served as President of the Student Body his senior year of high school before graduating in 1917 and was drafted along with his brother into the army at the beginning of WWI. There, he served as an army medic—the soldiers who carried wounded soldiers on stretchers.

At the beginning of the war, all medics were required to wear armbands as identifiers - white with a red cross. However, once the army realized made easy targets of the men, especially while carrying litters (stretchers with wounded soldiers), the armbands were discarded. The army then gave each of the medics a forty-five-caliber pistol, yet the guns were so heavy the men needed a plastic sac to carry them.

After the war, Jim's father along with his brother who'd also served, became part of the distinguished Rainbow division, which had been activated in August of 1917 and was comprised of soldiers who took part in one of the four major Operations in France: the Champagne-Marne, the Aisne-Marne, the Battle of Saint-Mihiel, and the Meuse-Argonne Offensive. Jim recalls this about the wartime stories his father told him.

"My dad said he may or may not have shot someone, but he said once an enemy soldier was so close to him, he's not sure how could he have missed when he shot his gun. He was a handsome guy, but he drank way too much and generally got into trouble in the army, mostly in France.

"Periodically, he would lose his stripes, but his brother just happened to be his commanding officer, so each time Frederic was able to earn them all back. He also played the bass drum in the army and loved music. He actually brought a first-bass violin back to the States when he returned from the war."

Jim recalled how growing up in Detroit was difficult and winters were bitterly cold. His father provided for his family well, but he was not very involved in the children's lives. He'd learned first to be a mortician. However, one day a friend told him that he'd never shake his hand again if Frederick stayed in the business because he wouldn't know where his hand had been. Frederick then went to work as an optician, though that decision didn't work well for him, either.

Jim's father eventually became a salesman for the Michigan Steel Tube Products company and travelled often for his work. Jim recalled more memories of their next-door neighbor, Mr. Briggs, than his father. Mr. Briggs took Jim under his wing as one of his own family, introduced him to fishing and hunting, and took him golfing at the greens in town. He would chip golf balls over the fence between their houses for Jim would catch in his mitt. Jim said much of what he learned about life and being a father, he learned from Mr. Briggs.

Music ran in the family as Jim's sister, Lorna Lou, began piano lessons at age four; she learned from a large and imposing teacher named Hazel Zumstein. By high school, Lorna Lou had taken on flute playing, as well. However, as a short girl just under five feet tall, the size of her hands proved too difficult for her to excel at the instrument.

"Our mother used to talk about the long parades the students in the band were in. And Lorna Lou was so short, she'd start out in the front row, but end up at the back of the line because her legs couldn't keep up."

"My father used to get such a kick of how the

spats for her boots would be covered up by her band uniform by the end of it, he would just laugh at her as she marched down the street behind everyone else."

It was a day like any other, the year was 1944, and Jim was nine years old when he experienced something that would prove to be a major turning point in his life. He and a few friends had gone down to Ives Field to watch a baseball game. It was an athletic park with tennis courts, basketball and a baseball diamond, and Jim loved to watch the games. The boys snuck under the fence to watch a game of donkey baseball; the Buckeyes were one of the pioneer promoters of the idea of playing various games from the backs of specially trained donkeys, for some fun, wholesome family entertainment. However, in the middle of the game, Jim started feeling sick and rushed back home.

On the way up to his room, his legs gave way. He screamed and grabbed his back from the pain. The next day, his father stayed home from work to take Jim to the local hospital, Highland Park General. There, the nurses put hot packs on him not knowing what else to do.

These actually caused more pain as they hadn't been properly rung out and induced boils all over his back. After three days of almost unbearable pain and no relief, Jim's father took him out of Highland Park and admitted Jim into the larger and more renowned, Henry Ford Hospital in Detroit, where that Jim received treatment and therapy.

His left leg had become permanently paralyzed and Jim had no idea what had happened. He stayed in the Henry

Ford hospital for five plua months, many days of which he experienced painful muscle spasms. It wasn't until three months into his stay, one slow Saturday morning, when he finally asked a nurse walking by his hospital bed what was wrong. She said polio, and when he didn't understand, she told him "infantile paralysis" which is how the disease was referred to then. He recalls yelling, "Shit, that's what FDR has!" because every child knew, the then-President had contracted the terrifying poliomyelitis disease.

Jim slowly learned to walk with the use of what was referred to as Canadian crutches—a type of crutch with a cuff at the top to go around the forearm, also known as the Lofstrand crutch, and used by inserting the arm into a cuff and holding the grip. He did not attend school that year and read a lot of comic books in the hospital. "Those books never left the hospital, no they were burned after we were done with them, given the contagiousness of the disease".

As part of his therapy, he also remembers being lowered into what is known as a Hubbard tank; a full-body immersion tank used for hydrotherapy. In the tank, he could paddle around and try to regain his muscle strength. During his stay there, Jim established camaraderie with the other children who were hospitalized.

After nearly six months of care, for which Jim's family had no medical insurance and somehow paid for out-of-pocket, his parents asked Jim's doctor what they should do next. In a hushed tone, he told them, if Jim was his own child, he would take Jim out of the hospital, to the 'Sister Elizabeth Kenny Institute' for rehabilitation. The doctor told them not to proceed with the surgery the other doctors had recommended.

The Sister Kenny Institute was located twelve hours drive away from home. He and his parents took trains there, changing trains in Chicago. They experienced multiple delays as troops were returning home from the war at the same time. Though the train ride was long and arduous, Jim's family met another family on it from Minneapolis. This family would play an integral part of Jim's stay in Michigan while at the Kenny Institute.

After they arrived, Jim was put into a nearby hospital for three days to ensure that he was no longer contagious, then admitted to the Institute, then his parents left him to go home. Jim would be stay in Sister Kenny's care for six more months with about sixteen other children while he underwent daily therapy for his polio affliction. The woman Jim knew as "Sister Kenny" was born Elizabeth Kenny in Australia in 1880. She had been trained as an army nurse and treated the sick for thirty-one years in the bushlands of Australia. She was then granted the honorific title "Sister" - used in Commonwealth countries for "nurse."

In 1911, when she encountered her first case of polio, Sister Kenny was unaware of the conventional polio treatment to immobilize the affected muscles with splints. Instead, she used common sense and her understanding of anatomy to treat the symptoms of the disease. By applying moist hot packs to help loosen muscles and relieve pain, she enabled limbs to be moved, stretched, and eventually strengthened.

The theory of her treatment was called muscle "re-education"; retraining muscles to function again. In 1940, Sister Kenny traveled to the US and eventually to Minneapolis, Minnesota and in 1942 where the Institute was established. Her pioneering principles of muscle rehabilitation became the foundation of physical therapy, and the Sister Kenny Rehabilitation Institute became one of the premier rehabilitation centers in the country, known for its progressive and innovative vision.

As for the family Jim met on their initial train ride, they came to visit him most every weekend at the Sister Kenny Institute, and they made the long time he spent there bearable although his own family wasn't around.

By the time Jim was discharged and able to return home, he was ten years old. He had to learned to walk again but walked slowly, fell often, and had to repeat that year of school. He couldn't return to the Henry Ford school, though, because it wasn't physically designed for someone on crutches.

Instead, he went to a special school which he recalled as "just damn spooky", where the fourth through the twelfth grades were all in one room. At some point, his father took him out and got him into a private school called the Detroit Country Day School. There, Jim had to repeat 5th grade, but he made great grades and finished the eighth grade there with a blue medal for academics.

The summer before his ninth grade, his family moved to Warren, Ohio for his father's job. Jim went to a new public high school, which was a difficult and depressing experience. He recalls being the only student of over thousand students with crutches, at a time when being popular, participating in sports, and girls meant everything to a teenager's life.

It was around this time, at the beginning of WWII, when Jim's half-brother, Freddie who was older by ten years, got drafted and was sent straight out of high school to the Navy. Freddie was on the Navy LST boat, #779, and stayed in the army for the duration of the war. Surprisingly he did not receive any wounds or injuries there, even though he participated in many combat experiences. He landed in and fought in Okinawa and in New Guinea.

In fact, Freddie came over on the same boat as the Marines who are depicted in the renowned photograph *Raising the Flag on Iwo Jima*, which was taken on February 23, 1945, by famed photographer Joe Rosenthal. The image depicts five United States Marines and a United States Navy corpsman raising a U.S. flag atop Mount Suribachi during the Battle of Iwo Jima. This photograph was later used by Felix de Weldon to sculpt the Marine Corps War Memorial, which was dedicated in 1954 to all Marines who died for their country past and present; it is located adjacent to Arlington National Cemetery just outside Washington, D.C.

It's interesting to note that Freddie was of borderline intelligence and yet the army still took him. While serving, despite Freddie's mental limitations, the other servicemen he served with never took advantage of him; in fact, they nearly made him the mascot of the unit. And after coming home, Freddie never seemed upset or bothered by all he witnessed in battle. For the rest of his life, he took simple jobs washing dishes in restaurants until he passed away.

In high school, Jim couldn't play sports, so he became involved with the drama club. He was also proud of being elected as President of the Student Body his senior year, just as his father had before him.

By this time, Mr. Briggs, the neighbor next door had taught Jim many new activities he could do despite his physical limitations, including shooting guns at the range and learning to drive a car (automatic, not a stick shift). Jim also had a girlfriend, a fellow student from down the street.

He graduated from high school with stellar grades that helped land him in Allegany College in Pennsylvania the next year. At Allegany, he joined the SAE (Sigma Alpha Epsilon) fraternity, though he became the first student there to deactivate in preparation for medical school because of the negative reputation fraternities had acquired. He did become very good at ping-pong and made his mark on campus winning game after game against other students. At Allegany, Jim was chosen to serve as a Student Counselor, even as a sophomore.

Jim enjoyed college much more than high school, and unfortunately his grades at Alleghany reflected his extracurricular activities. But he was determined to go on to med school. Without a nigh G.P.A., a friend recommended Jim to request an in-person interview with his application and grade submission, given his physical disability. Jim did and was immediately accepted; he always joked, it was his personality that secured his college enrollment. He was accepted into medical school in Cleveland, Ohio at Western Reserve University.

It was back at Alleghany, though, where he met his first wife. Jeneva "Ginny" Smith and Jim dated until her senior year, when she quit to go home to work on her family's farm in New York. Although Ginny never returned to school, the couple continued to date, and she followed him to Cleveland when he went to medical school. They were married at the end of his first year, and Ginny worked as a secretary in the local hospital during his schooling.

Though the couple had three daughters together, they divorced after ten years. Later, Jim would meet his second wife, Sandy, to whom he was married for more than thirty years. After completing his residency in Oklahoma City, he set up a practice in the field of psychiatry at the VA Hospital in Tacoma, Washington.

Eventually, he and Sandy who had a Master's in Psychiatric Nursing, moved to Oklahoma City, and finally to Charleston, SC where Jim lives today. Sandy has since passed away. As for Jim's daughters: Kathy lives in Moncks Corner, SC; Linda lives in Rock Hill, NC; and Amy lives near Charlotte, NC. Jim has long been confined to a wheelchair at Summit Place but is proud of the adversity he overcame and all he has accomplished.

Sumter, South Carolina - November 1927

Barbara (Dukes) Grant

Barbara Grant was born in Sumter, South Carolina. Her mother, Irene Hamilton Dukes, was an easy-going woman and a wonderful cook. Barbara recalled with fondness that her mother's food was delicious, though always fried, "of course." Irene was a good woman who never complained about anything, and Barbara was the youngest of her three children, all a few years apart in age.

While she, her sister and brother were at school, their mother played bridge and took care of the house during the day. And she was always there when the kids got home. As for Barbara's father, Charles Dukes, he was a good man, not strict like many fathers of the era. She said this about her family and childhood:

> "We were good kids, and we didn't disobey our parents much at all. Of course, there were no drugs back then like you see now, and it was a terrible thing if a girl got pregnant, so kids and young people just didn't do the things they do today. My brother and sister and I, we all did mostly what we were told."

One of Barbara's favorite memories is when her father took her on a trip to Washington one weekend when she was in the seventh grade. Her mother had a cousin, Gladys, whose husband was stationed in the service there, and Gladys took Barbara shopping at Best & Co., an upscale children's clothing retailer that operated from 1879 to 1971. There, Gladys bought Barbara a beautiful, white and pink polka-dot dress, and together they toured the shops of the city.

Back home, Barbara's family often visited Bennettsville, South Carolina, the town where her mother's family was from, which was about an hour and a half away. Founded in 1819 and named after Governor Thomas Bennett, Bennettsville grew into one of the richest agricultural communities in the state. Legend has it, the land was once so rich, it was sold by the pound instead of the acre. The state of South Carolina recognized Bennettsville's prominence by officially designating it South Carolina's "first" Great Town, and its lifestyle and affluence are captured by the many Victorian and Greek revival homes and public buildings there.

When Barbara was young, their family moved away from Sumter to Spartanburg for her father's job; he was a cotton buyer for the Palmetto Cotton Company. They lived there until the seventh grade, and she made many friends in Spartanburg. When she moved again, her friends threw her a huge going-away party at the local bowling alley. Afterward, they all went to her close friend, Nathalie Walker's, house for ice cream sundaes. Barbara recalls it as a memorable day, despite the sadness at moving away from her friends. Her favorite and closest friends from Spartanburg, she managed to stay in touch with for years and years until the time when the women all got married and had kids of their own.

From Spartanburg, the family moved to Columbia and stayed there for the remainder of Barbara's childhood. There, she took dancing lessons from the well-respected Ms. Isabel Sloane, who taught dance in town for many years. She enjoyed all the dances—ballroom, jitterbug and tap— but she was active in high school, as well. There were a number of school clubs to choose from, but in those days, one would have to be invited into them, a girl couldn't simply join just because she wished.

"For young girls, it was one of those situations where if you'd didn't get invited in, you went home and cried," Barbara recalled. Le Coquettes was one particular popular girls' group; Doc Hosman was its counter group for the boys. Le Coquettes members enjoyed barn dances twice a year, ran bake sales and participated in local community activities.

Then the year before Barbara's junior year, in August of 1942, she made the local papers because of a swimming accident. She was at the Forest Lake Country Club with her best friend, Jean, who jumped on top of Barbara in the pool which caused a fracture in her neck. Fortunately, Barbara fully recovered from the incident. "We never told anyone what really happened in the pool that day. I said she was just playing around because I didn't want get my dear friend in trouble."

In high school, several local stores would ask the taller, pretty girls to model their clothes, and Tapp's Department Store asked Barbara to model for them on a number of occasions. Though the first Tapp's store was located in Dalton, Georgia in 1890, Tapp's was a very distinctive store in downtown Columbia. Completed in 1940, it featured a streamlined modern design and was the first department store east of the Mississippi to offer an air-conditioned shopping experience *and* a restaurant in the basement level.

Another time, she and her friends went to Myrtle Beach to model for the Elizabeth Wolf Store. However, unlike the high price tags attached with modeling today, the girls were never given a dime for the dozen for the modeling jobs they offered to do.

In 1944, Barbara graduated from Columbia High School, then went to Brenau College in Gainesville, Georgia to study English. She recalls that almost everyone smoked back then. Her "suite mates" (now referred to as dorm roommates) taught Barbara how to roll her own cigarettes, though fortunately she never picked up the habit. After one year at Brenau, she transferred to the University of South Carolina to be closer to home. She was active in college and served as Vice President of her senior class in the school's student body.

After graduation, Barbara started teaching English classes for seventh and eighth graders in nearby Bishopville. Her friend, Isabel, went with her one day to see if she could get a job there, as well. Isabelle was dating a man named David Johnson who'd brought his friend, Thomas "McDonald" Lyles, along for the ride. Though Barbara was already dating another guy at the time, she liked Donald as soon as they met and the two started to date. They "went together" for about six months before Barbara married Donald in 1948.

The couple soon moved to Donald's hometown of Winnsboro, where she went to work for the Department of

Welfare. Their first daughter, Helen, was born a year later. Donald was well-liked in town, and the couple never missed a Carolina football game. Donald had also attended USC, though he was seven years older and graduated before Barbara attended. Immediately after graduation, he was drafted into the war as a bombardier in the Air Force, and though he rarely talked about his experiences, he did share with Barbara that he flew more than thirty missions, primarily over Germany and England.

Upon returning from the war, Donald co-owned a store with his father called Lyles & Lyles Grocery, but the business didn't do well, and they eventually sold it. Barbara and Donald then moved from Winnsboro to Greenwood where Donald accepted a job as manager of the cotton warehouse with the Textile Bonded Storage Company, owned by Abney Mills.

In this occupation, her father would have been referred to as a "linthead" in the day, a Southern term used to describe white people who worked with cotton in a textile mill. This title addresses the fragments of cotton that stick in the hair and on the clothing of the mill managers as they patrol the factory.

Their first daughter, Helen, was five years old and Barbara (their second daughter) was an infant when the family moved to Greenwood. For their family, Donald and Barbara decided to settle there. They stayed in Greenwood for twenty-five years so the girls could live out their childhoods in one place. Barbara took a job as a case worker in town for what was originally called the Welfare Department, then later renamed the Department of Public

Services. The organization primarily handled child abuse cases, young pregnancies, and disabled cases; she worked there for forty years, eventually serving as the County Director of the organization. Barbara had this to say about her work and the era:

> "Our office helped girls who were in trouble. It was all in secret back then, no one even talked about who the fathers were. It was so hush-hush. There was a place the girls went to in Columbia, they stayed there until the baby was born. After, they'd put the babies up for adoption and the girls would just go back home."

And in the 1970's, the local paper published this about Barbara's accolades at her job:

> "Barbara serves as President of the Palladian Study Club. She spoke at their recent meeting, discussing the Alliance for Progress in Latin America - a product of the Kennedy Administration that was planned as a ten-year undertaking designed to stimulate economic growth and sociological change in the country."

She made the papers more over the years and one final time when she served as Director of the Greenwood County Department of Social Services and was commended for coordinating efforts to provide preventative and complete medical services to eligible individuals in the community.

Barbara and Donald's daughter, Helen, attended Queens College in Charlotte, North Carolina, which was then an all-girls school. For college, daughter Barbara first went to Converse College in Spartanburg which is a private liberal arts college for women, and then transferred after a year to Clemson because Converse didn't offer a degree in the field of Engineering.

> "Oh, I remember a funny story when Helen was getting ready for college. She wanted us to get one of those bedrest things with arm rests that you put it on your bed. We used to call them 'husbands' back then. Well, Donald I went to Tapp's Department store to see if they had one. There was a crowd at the elevator, so I just took the stairs up and he waited for me downstairs.
>
> Well, I just went all the way up and when I opened the door at the top floor, I looked around and realized I was stuck on the roof of the building! And before I could gather my wits, the door shut and locked behind me. I yelled for help for an hour before finally one of the employees finally heard me. When he opened the door to the roof and asked me what I was doing up there, I shouted, *'I'm looking for a husband, of course!'*, which brought a confused look to the young man's face."

Barbara and Donald were married for forty-three years before he died of throat cancer after tragically having his voice box removed one year earlier. She'd been widowed for ten years when she met someone new. She shared a condo at Litchfield by the Sea near Pawley's Island with some friends; Litchfield-by-the-Sea is a beachside community in the heart of the South Carolina Low Country located south of Myrtle Beach and north of historic Georgetown. One day, she met a man who co-owned another unit down the hall.

"Apparently, he'd called down to the gate to ask them for my phone number, but they wouldn't give it to him. He argued with them for so long, they finally did. It was nearly a year later when Don Dubose Grant and I were married, in 1997.

"Don was an Engineer by schooling but had returned to help run the farm with his father at D.D. Grant & Son Farm. It was a large farm, about 2500 acres and they mainly grew cotton, corn and tobacco. I think it was those chemicals they'd used on the farm that gave him cancer. Very sad.

"Don was an only child and a wonderful husband who treated me very well. I didn't even need to worry about cooking for someone again after I'd been a widow for ten years. He told me not to worry about it, that he'd cook for me or take me out. We were married for six years before he, too, died of cancer."

After Don passed away, Barbara was able go on some amazing trips around the world. One in particular was to

Hong Kong, China with her daughter, Barbara. Together, they went on the cruise ship, 'The World'—the only private residential community-at-sea where residents can travel the globe without ever leaving home. On it, mother and daughter toured mainland China, then flew back home a few weeks later. Barbara also spent two weeks in Mexico one summer at a lovely house with a full-service staff and pool. She has wonderful memories of her time spent abroad and cherishes those moments in her life.

As an aside, Barbara remembers a very attractive water pitcher that accompanied her family during each of their moves. The pitcher was always prominently displayed, and Barbara's grandmother in Bennettsville told her she'd purchased the pitcher years before at historic Jamestown; the Jamestown historic district is where the English first disembarked from their ships in 1652, which is how they came to settle in what was then known as Charlestown. Unfortunately, the family doesn't know where the pitcher is but assume it holds great value and are in the process of trying to locate the family heirloom.

Though Barbara's husbands are both gone, her two daughters are dear to her and stayed close by; daughter Barbara lives in Atlanta, and Helen lives in Charleston. And of those five, close friend from Barbara's childhood days in Spartanburg, just one is still here. The 'girls' stay in touch as often as they can. Her one sister died of cancer at the young age of 57; their brother passed away at the age of ninety from Alzheimer's a few years ago.

Barbara Grant-Lyles is a distinguished and accomplished woman who made the papers a number of times throughout her life; for her modeling work, her swimming accident, and the many accomplishments in her career. After suffering a stroke in 2008, she now resides at Summit Place. She left a mark in her community and looks back on her life, her marriages and her children with great fondness and pride.

Oklahoma City, Oklahoma - August 1917

Anne (Graham) Raynes

Anne Graham was born in Oklahoma City, Oklahoma, a city nearly perfectly equidistant from Los Angeles and New York. It is also where the world's first parking meter was installed, on July 16, 1935, and where the first shopping cart was invented.

Anne's parents both grew up downtown. Her father, Garrett Graham, became a minister and was the epitome of a true Baptist preacher. He was a strict and hard man; he expected a great deal from his wife and children. Anne's mother, Lillian, appropriately served her role as the pastor's wife and obediently did whatever her husband requested during those years Anne and her siblings grew up at home.

> "When we kids were off at school, I think my momma just cleaned and cooked. She worked hard and she was a good mother for us. I don't remember her doing much of anything else except taking care of us kids and the home, bless her heart."

As the preacher's family, the Raynes resided in the local parsonages; a parsonage is a home owned by the church, specifically used to provide housing for the town's minister. These dwellings date back to the Middle Ages, when the parish priest would lodge in a room over the church porch, though by the twelfth century a separate parsonage house had become more common.

In England after the first World War, the Church of England began to recognize that maintaining large parsonages suitable for big Victorian families with their servants was quite impractical. And by 1925, at least a fifth of parsonages were considered oversized, so during the twentieth century churches sold some 10,000 parsonages and replaced them in many cases with smaller ones. Though pastors and ministers today often receive a housing supplement with their role as head of the church, parsonage dwellings are now mostly a thing of the past.

Anne was the oldest child, with two sisters and two brothers, and a two-year difference between each child.

The family did not have much, certainly not many extras, but their mother always made sure to serve the family three hot meals a day. They moved around often as her father was called to serve in different churches over the years, so Anne and her siblings lived in different towns and cities throughout her childhood.

She said they were quickly identified as the "preacher's kids" every time they came to a new town, and wherever they went, the Raynes children were expected to be on their best behavior. All during her childhood, the kids had to be at church every Sunday and behave well, even more than any other time during their childhood years.

> "It wasn't a good thing to misbehave. Daddy gave us a whipping with his hand or a belt if we did, so you only did it once and then you learned. The boys weren't as good as the girls. It seemed, they always managed to get themselves into trouble. It was tough, I can tell you, as we always tried to be the perfect kids."

Anne was kept on "a tight leash" by her parents, even in high school. She wasn't allowed to dance, she didn't go to the movies, or engage in extra-curricular activities, even those available through school. "The Baptist were just so strict, and they expected too much of their minister's children back then."

The family's last move occurred just before Anne graduated from high school when they relocated to Virginia. Her father served as pastor there for many years for the Euclid Avenue Baptist Church in nearby Bristol.

Bristol's central location and convenient transportation connections made it the center of the five-state area. State Street joins Tennessee and Virginia, and puts the states of West Virginia, Kentucky, and North Carolina within easy driving distance. The Euclid Avenue Southern Baptist church has served the local communities for over eighty-five years.

Ironically, Anne would have attended the same school as her future husband in Virginia, but it didn't offer the subjects she needed to graduate after their many family moves. Instead, she enrolled in the school across the river in Bristol, in the same town where her father was the pastor.

Fate is what allowed the two to meet, when one day she and one of her brothers were walking down the street to check out the new town and George had come out with his nephew to meet the new preacher's kids. Anne recalls this of the day she and George met:

> "Oh, I thought he was just a doll, and I was instantly smitten. I found out his name was George, and we soon started to date. Of course, we weren't allowed to go to many places together while still in high school, only to ball games and functions at church or school. And everything we did was watched. Honestly, we just couldn't wait to graduate and go out on our own."

After high school, Anne enrolled in the junior program at Mars Hill Junior College in Charlotte, a Baptist School and the oldest school in western North Carolina. From 1859 to 2013, the school went by the name of Mars Hill College, then in August 2013 it officially changed its name to Mars Hill University.

Anne obtained her degree after two years, while George attended Kings College which also later changed its name to King University. He continued school and obtained a bachelor's degree in Business. The couple were married as soon as George graduated, and although they didn't have a true honeymoon, they did get to the beach for a weekend, which was the start of a long and happy life together.

"George was just wonderful, the dearest, sweetest, kindest man, and a very loving husband. He loved our children, and we loved our lives. He was happy and so was I. Gosh, he was so handsome, and even my daddy liked him. Sometimes I just couldn't believe he was mine. George was the best thing that happened to me."

Once George finished his schooling, he went into the insurance business and eventually owned/ran his own insurance agency, Raynes Insurance. Anne started working as a teller at a bank and worked her way up to lead trainer for all tellers hired.

After numerous mergers and acquisitions, she worked for the now Bank of America, solely responsible for hiring tellers and facilitating training. She loved her job and worked for twenty years before retiring. She was also actively involved with the local Rotary, a worldwide service of 1.2 million-plus members, focused on building better communities and changing lives.

The couple had four children during their forty-plus years of marriage. Mel, their first child, lives in Lawrence, Kansas. Karen lives in Mt. Pleasant, and Mark lives in Gaylax, Virginia. And Andrew, who had settled down in their hometown of Charlotte, and sadly died three years ago of a sudden heart attack.

Anne was never close with her brothers after she married, and they all went their separate ways. They have both since passed away: the youngest died years ago and the other just last year. Of her two sisters, Onelda and Roselle, one lives on Lake Norman near Charlotte, and the other lives in Florida.

But Anne and George stayed in Charlotte for the duration of their children's young lives; quite opposite the experience of Anne's own childhood, moving around from town-to-town and exactly the kind of childhood she wanted for them.

And after the kids grew up and left, she and George traveled around the country before he passed away in September, 1994 at sixty-five. Today, Anne is an active resident at Summit Place. She has a wonderful, matter-of-fact outlook on her life and spoke of her past and her family with great fondness, without regret.

Jamestown, New York - August 1925

Robert "Bob" Elf

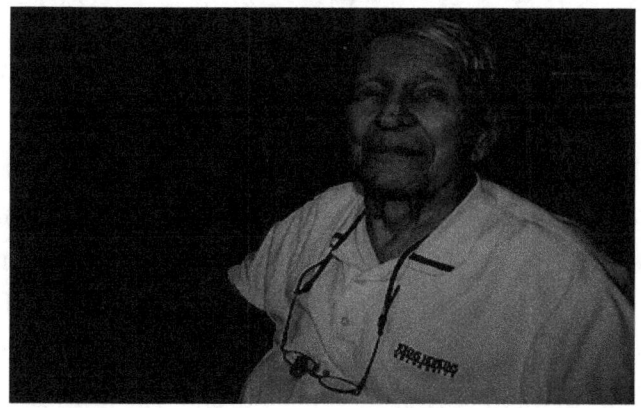

Bob Elf was born in Jamestown, New York in August, 1925. His mother, Signa, was born in the United States. However his father's family had come over from Sweden on a boat when he was just six years old. Most Swedish immigrants who immigrated to the States headed to New York, Massachusetts, or inland to Ohio—all areas of the country that most resembled their native homelands.

Many industrial workers settled around Jamestown, New York, an area which attracted hundreds of Swedish immigrants over the years. The Fenton History Center located in Jamestown is a cultural institution that offers genealogy reports for interested Swedish families and descendants.

Bob's father, Sven, had three brothers and three sisters; John, Esther, Carl, Milton, Sarah, and Nells. Sven was the second to youngest of the seven children. He was given a common Swedish name, yet when the officials at Ellis Island registered their family, his name was either misunderstood or misspelled and Sven became "Swan." And "Swannie" was his nickname for the rest of life.

Growing up, Bob's father was a dominant figure in their family's lives; Swannie led his role as ruler of the house to the fullest. He did not allow Signa, the boys' mother to drive a car, and as a stay-at-home mother she had no income of her own. If she needed any clothing or even items for the house, she had to ask her husband for the money and sometimes ask him for a ride into town to shop. And she always brought her purchases home for his approval before she was allowed to keep them.

Both of Bob's parents both came from large families, as his mother was one of six siblings. Because of the hardships they each experienced growing up, the couple decided to have only two children of their own and "leave it at that". Bob's younger brother by two and a half years was Frederick and the boys were close.

The extended family, however, with all of the aunts and uncles who lived nearby in the same community, did not get along well. Bob remembers quibbling and arguing between them, so he and his brother decided as young children, they would be mindful to their parents and help keep peace in the home. As adults, the brothers got along well and enjoyed a wonderful and loving sibling relationship through the years.

Their father worked as a tool engineer for the Dahlstrom Metallic Door Company for many years to support his family. The company was founded by Charles Peter Dahlstrom who came from the island of Gotland, Sweden, and had immigrated to the United States back in 1891 after learning the trade of tool and die-making. With a very inventive mechanical mind, Charles was noted in his time for his genius in devising improvements on machinery. Charles eventually made his way to Jamestown, where he created a new metallic door and obtained the patent for it. This invention is what served as the start of the Dahlstrom company in 1904, and his doors would soon be installed in hotels and schools nationwide.

During the years of the Depression when Bob and his brother were young, Swan Elf was able to maintain his employment with Dalhstrom only because he agreed to work the night shift, instead. Bob remembers this about those early, difficult days:

> "We were not well-off, but in the early 30's survival was the chief concern. We had food on the table, but not much. Back in Sweden, fish was the main source of food and my dad loved it, even my mother did. But Frederick and I always hated fish. Chicken was a once a week delicacy, though now people eat it so often, it's much different."

Though Bob and his brother went to Sunday School growing up, Bob doesn't remember his parents attending the service. Music, however, was a big part of their lives and their home had an extra room that housed a piano. Aunt Esther gave the children weekly music lessons, as she was an accomplished pianist and organist who'd graduated from the Jamestown Conservatory and quickly became known in the local music scene for her musical talents. Besides piano, the only other activity Bob was able to participate in was badminton. This is because he was born with a hernia, and in those days a hernia was a physical complication that required a serious surgical procedure.

The first hernia operation was actually performed as early as 1777, albeit unsuccessfully. Then in 1916, a Polish surgeon had a 'somewhat' successful operation, as the patient died after, not during the procedural attempt to perform hernia surgery. However, it wasn't until Dr. Chester McVay performed the surgery in 1942, when it became a more routine operation in the U.S. This was about the same time Bob finished high school, and during the start of WWII. It was also around the time that he saw his future wife at school one day.

"I saw her coming down a flight of stairs and thought, 'Wow, that is some good-looking woman!' Though we were at the same school, Joyce had grown up in a different part of town, so we never knew each other. The very first day I saw her, I arranged for us to meet through a good friend. Soon, we started dating. We were juniors in high school, still just kids, really."

Because it was wartime, all the young men faced the draft that year. Bob knew he wanted to enlist in the Navy instead to become an Air Cadet. However, he also knew the military would never take him with his hernia condition. So, Bob took the initiative and talked to a Naval doctor. At the doctor's advice, he proceeded to schedule the still relatively new surgical procedure to be performed over Christmas break of his senior year. Back then, this surgery took two weeks to recover from—today it is performed as an out-patient operation and patients are discharged the same day.

After a successful operation, Bob was able to enter the Navy. He was eighteen; the year was 1943. He was immediately sent to Pensacola, Florida to begin the long, step-by-step process of training to become an aviator. He eventually completed his training there and was sent to Colgate University in central New York classified as a Naval Air Cadet. There, he was paired up with fellow cadet, Otto Graham, because they were physically the same size and academically at a similar level. Together, they passed all of the tests and completed their training, before being sent off to flight school.

Otto was later sent to Iowa, while Bob went to Allentown-Bethlehem, Pennsylvania. Otto would later become an All-American basketball and football player at Northwestern, and was the main quarterback for the Cleveland Browns, earning himself the record in the Hall of Fame for sports.

And Pennsylvania is, finally, where Bob learned how to fly. However, one afternoon, in the final part of his flight training, he was playing touch-football and tripped over someone on the field while catching a pass. He landed on his wrist, breaking many bones. This would be the first of a few accidental injuries he would sustain in flight school. From Pennsylvania, with a cast on his arm, he was sent to North Carolina, then to Chicago, Illinois, and finally to Idaho. It was there that the Navy determined surgery needed to be performed on Bob's wrist.

After the operation, he was sent back to North Carolina and this time to Chapel Hill, where he recuperated and continued his training. This involved a survival course on how to navigate and recognize approaching enemy aircraft; a twenty-week program offering ten elective sports of which they had to participate in two. Bob chose boxing and football, and subsequently suffered another unfortunate accident with his wrist while boxing one day. This was the second time he broke his wrist. Then soon after, while tackling someone in football, he dislocated his shoulder.

With another cast on his wrist, Bob could no longer properly navigate or perform the required pilot tests. At this point in his training, the Navy sent him to Chicago, Illinois to recuperate. After staying there several months, he was then sent to the naval hospital in Ashville, North Carolina, and finally in Houston, Texas. To note, all of these military relocations and assignments occurred by train back then. The military didn't fly soldiers nearly as often as they do today, so the trips were lengthy and time-consuming. On that trip to Texas, he saw a sign near the tracks in South Carolina that read: "Sailors and Dogs stay away!", and Bob really thinking, *Okay, I won't stay*, though ironically, South Carolina is where he eventually would end up living.

Despite the painful bone graft surgery Bob endured, his wrist did not properly heal and would permanently remain an issue. Bob was discharged from the Navy in 1946 for medical reasons, deemed unable to competently fly a plane, and returned home. His brother, who had opted into the Marine Corps, was stationed in Iowa and remained there for his schooling. And as close as they remained, Bob and his brother would never live in the same town again.

Though disappointed to end his service, Bob was anxious to return home to Joyce, the woman whom he'd dated in high school. He headed back to Jamestown, New York. Joyce was seventy miles away in Buffalo completing her nurses' training. Then, women could either become nurses or teachers, so when Bob left for the Navy training, Joyce had entered the nurses' training program located in Buffalo. At the start, there were 120 students in her class; 20 left because they were homesick, and in the end barely 50 graduated from the program.

The couple started dating again after he returned and soon wanted to get married. However, in those days, if a woman in nurses' training got married, they would be kicked out of the program. So, the couple made plans to secretly but legally marry. The private ceremony was performed on December 6, 1946, with just five people in attendance, and they didn't announce the wedding until after Joyce had graduated on St. Patrick's Day of the following year.

As a graduate nurse, while Joyce was waiting for her R.N. designation, she worked primarily with patients who had contracted polio; this was solely a volunteer job, considering the concern and fear about the contagiousness of the disease. It was on Friday, July 13th of the same year in 1947, when she finally received the letter stating she was officially a Registered Nurse. The very same day, Bob received a letter stating his acceptance into the University of North Carolina.

Though rooms for couples to rent near the University were scarce, Bob found one for them that would be one of many as time went on for the newly married couple. The first rented room had no kitchen, and they shared a bathroom with the house owners; privacy was scarce. They were also told up front that if Joyce got pregnant, they would have to move out and find a new place to live. Bob recalled this with a chuckle:

"Well, sure enough despite our quite limited circumstances and the warning, Joyce did get pregnant. It took me a while to find a place to take her in, let alone take a couple that would soon have a child. I eventually found an apartment and our daughter, Lee Caroline, was born, in 1948.

"I finished college with a Bachelor's of Science in Marketing, then went on to law school at Duke University, there were just fifty students in my class.

"Our son, Bryon, would be born a few years later in 1954 after I finished law school. Those were different days, that's for sure, and it was hell on wheels for a long time for Joyce and me, trying to make things work. Really, we were just trying to survive."

Joyce worked in the local city hospital seeing up to forty-five patients at time. Walking around with a waistband of drugs, she administered them to patients (quite unlike the bedside methods in hospitals today). While Bob attended law school at Duke University, Joyce went into private duty at the University Hospital for just ten dollars a day. After law school, Bob eventually took a job with McBee Systems, selling manual business forms. Though he had a large territory, they were "as poor as church mice" in those early years.

One day, he realized, he would need to show the company how to do things differently in order to get somewhere. This is exactly what he did. He created a system and sold his new accounting and records-keeping systems to local businesses. Eventually, there were more than two hundred offices using Bob's checking paper system by the time he left his position. He flew often for his work, and when McBee offered him the job of District Manager based out of Charlotte, North Carolina ("Which was just a little cow-town back then," he joked), he accepted.

McBee Systems soon became Royal McBee and finally Litton. While there, a guy from Xerox saw the potential Bob had created—a one-system process that could capture all the money transactions. Together they obtained contracts with all the local schools and hospitals to use their system. Unfortunately, as District Manager Bob was not eligible for the grossly huge sales commissions, though he and Joyce were given an all-expenses paid trip to Europe.

At some point, Joyce decided she'd rather live near the beach, so the couple sold their home in Charlotte and headed to Atlantic Beach near Jacksonville, Florida. There they bought a beautiful, custom-made and very unique home near the ocean that the family still owns today; the couple's son Bryon would later attend Florida State. Collecting sharks' teeth soon became a hobby, and the couple had a local artist create a design with all the teeth they'd gathered, and put them in one beautiful piece of artwork.

When asked about the 'best' part of his long and accomplished life, Bob said this with a smile:

"Marrying my girlfriend, because it opened the door for so many things closed to us while growing up. Neither of us could wait to get away, and we both wanted more.

When we lived in Jacksonville, it was such a good time. We loved the beach, and Joyce used to collect shark teeth (made into a lovely piece of art and framed) every time we went to the ocean. Those were good days, I'll tell you... just really, good days."

Bob has had several major surgeries over the years, yet his left hand still remains broken. Though the game of golf was always a big part of their family lives, he was at least able to learn the sport. Joyce took lessons a few times, but eventually decided golf wasn't for her. It was their daughter and son who learned a love for the game; together they all enjoyed watching the Master's each year.

Bob admitted that both he and Joyce smoked for the better part of their fifty years together ("Well, everyone did back then."), and sadly Joyce contracted lung cancer in 2007. Not wishing to undergo chemotherapy, she passed away just two months after her diagnosis. Their son, Byron and his wife live in Gainesville, Florida, while Lee, who attended Columbia College in South Carolina, lives in Charleston with her husband (ironically, also named 'Lee'). Bob resides in Summit Place; he looks forward to their visits, watching golf and talking about the good old days.

Indianapolis, Indiana - September 1925

Carolyn (Knuth) Matthews

Carolyn Knuth was born in September of 1925, and grew up in Indianapolis, Indiana. Indianapolis city was planned by Alexander Ralston, who apprenticed under Pierre L'Enfant, the French architect who designed Washington D.C. It is the only major city in the United States not located on a river.

Carolyn was a 'surprise' baby who arrived late in her parents' lives; her mother was well in her forties when Carolyn was born. They lived in a big house on a hill located on Brookside Avenue. There were four other children; a sister more than twenty years older and three brothers, the youngest of whom was older by thirteen years. Though with the age gaps, she grew up more as an only child, Carolyn always felt there were always people around for her. Her sister even assisted their family doctor when Carolyn was born, in the kitchen of their family home. "My sister, Minnie, was already married by then. It was funny, but after I was born, everyone thought I was her baby!"

Their parents were both of German descent. Bertha Wilamena Nichols was known to be sweet and kind while Albert Carl Knuth, their father, was rather stern and aloof. Everyone spoke German at home, yet by the time Carolyn came along, no one in the family bothered to teach her their native language.

They all attended a church where the sermons were in German, yet only knowing a few words here and there, she never understood what the preacher was saying. At some point during WWII, however, as American soldiers fought against the Nazis overseas, churches in the United States stopped preaching in German and German immigrants limited their native conversations to the privacy of their homes.

"When the preacher used to speak in German at church, my mother would just turn around and give me a tablet and a pencil, so I'd have something to do. Once they stopped preaching in German, my poor dad couldn't understand a single word of those sermons, anymore, let alone sing along with the hymns. I know it was a hard life for my daddy here in the States, without knowing much English."

Unable to proficiently speak the tongue of the land, Carolyn's father found work he could do as a machinist for the railroad. However, when the Depression hit (1929 - 1933), he lost his job and had no choice but to go work for the Works Progress Administration, or the WPA. The WPA was one of the many programs initiated by the federal government under President Franklin D. Roosevelt. Its intent was to combat the devastating effects of the Great Depression by providing large-scale national works programs for what they referred to as 'jobless employables'—individuals to perform small useful projects in towns and cities for small pay. Carolyn recalls this about that time in her family life:

> "Men were always outside building parks and recreational areas everywhere around town, walk-throughs and trails. My daddy wasn't used to doing all that outside work in the yards, though, shoveling dirt and constructing things. I remember how sunburned his neck would be when he came home at night.
>
> "The WPA often provided food for the workers and their families, but it was mostly fruit. Oh my goodness, they had so much fruit— oranges, apples, bananas—mother used to make 'ades (lemonades, limeades…) with it all! Some days, I felt like I never wanted to see another piece of fruit again."

Carolyn's mother, Bertha, worked just as hard as their father, in taking care of the home. She raised all her own children, and later when one of Carolyn's brothers moved into the house next door with his family, she helped take care of those children, as well. She was quiet and kind, and Carolyn said she doesn't remember her mother getting mad about anything. She cooked all the time, mostly German foods like potato salads, meats and Spätzle or Knöpfle (soft, thick noodles); much of what she cooked was all in one big pot.

"The thing I remember my mom doing most, though, was the washing. We had a basement in our house, and she had her washing machine in the basement. There was no faucet down there, so she had to haul big water buckets downstairs. It was always early in the morning, before any of us would even be up. She'd have one big bucket for washing and one for rinsing, and I know she carried those heavy containers of water downstairs by herself, every day."

Despite their hard lives, her parents were married for many years and happy. Their local church, St. Peter's Lutheran Church, was significant in their family lives; the kids attended parochial school there through the seventh grade. Carolyn did not participate in any sports activities after school, only because she didn't like them.

What she loved most was being outdoors. She recalls spending her most of after-school hours riding a bicycle around town with her friends. Sometimes, they would ride across town to visit her elder sister, Minnie, and her family.

Carolyn loved seeing the birds, smelling the flowers and spending her time appreciating nature.

Though she recalls a good life while growing up, there were some unfortunate circumstances that befell Carolyn's family, as well as to Carolyn herself over the years. One of her brothers contracted polio. At its peak in the 1940's and 1950's, polio paralyzed or killed over half a million people worldwide each year. The polio vaccine would not be administered until years later, in February of 1954, in Philadelphia, Pennsylvania. Afterward, cases of polio in the United States dropped from under 15,000 in 1955 to less than 6,000 in 1956. By 1959, some ninety other countries were using the vaccine Dr. Jonas Salk had discovered.

As for Caroline's family, after her brother's affliction the entire family had to go into quarantine for months. Their groceries were delivered, house guests were forbidden, and no one was allowed to leave except her father for work. They eventually had to put her brother in the hospital to try to help get him better. He became temporarily paralyzed in one leg, but fortunately, he never had to go into what is referred to as the "iron lung".

There was no device more closely associated with the polio disease than the tank respirator, better known as the "iron lung". Created by two Harvard graduates in 1927, it was a negative pressure ventilator that enables a person to breathe when normal muscle control has been lost, or the work of breathing exceeds the person's ability. The machine could be seen in hospitals across the States, as the polio virus swept through towns and cities for decades before the vaccination was administered.

Eventually, Carolyn's brother was released from the hospital and sent home. Their mother encouraged him and pushed him hard to do the most he could, despite his physical limitations. "She would tell him, even if he had to crawl across the floor, to pull himself up to get something he needed for himself. She made him do it and it helped him heal." Carolyn recalls that he was able to pull one leg forward while the other he would drag behind him, but somehow over time he managed to walk and get stronger.

Ludwig (Luke), though at the age of eighteen was struck by polio when polio was at its height, grew older, got married and lived until his fifties before he suffered a heart attack as a result of the lifelong toll on his body.

During this time, Carolyn attended the same local, public high school as did her siblings before her, Arsenal Technical High—a school that was originally a true U.S. Civil War Arsenal. The arsenal closed down after the Spanish-American War (April - August 1898), but most of the original buildings from the Arsenal still remained intact, including the actual Arsenal building, the officer's Residence, the soldier's Barracks, the entrance Guardhouse, the Barn, and the Powder Magazine. The school was quite a change after the small private Christian school of her elementary days.

> "After being at our tiny Lutheran school for elementary, Arsenal was a difficult adjustment. It's where I met my husband, though, on "Hello Day." It was the opportunity to meet different students in school, all the kids wore a name tag.

"When Howard saw mine, he came up to me and asked if he could walk me home from school. That was the first day we were together, and I think were both in love from the start."

Though her father was a strict man, he liked Howard as much as her mother and took right to him. After graduating from high school, Carolyn worked at the local telephone company, and eventually the couple married. She worked until she became pregnant with their first child and had to leave her job.

"Back then, women just didn't work when they were pregnant, so at four months along, I had to quit my job. It's not like it is now, where pregnant women just show their bellies off and wear whatever they like. In our day, you didn't dress like that, and you didn't keep working once your baby was showing."

Howard attended a local trade school for a few years, but he mostly worked different jobs, and Carolyn said he always "worked hard, and worked a lot". Even back in high school, he'd had to seek work because his father, Charles, had an accident on the job and could no longer work to support their family.

Charles was a house painter, and he'd fallen off of a tall ladder one day, severely injuring his brain. In effect, she said, "he lost his mind" and the family had to put him in what they then referred to as an "insane hospital", or what is now called a mental institution. His father passed away a few years before Carolyn met Howard, so she never got to meet him.

Howard served in the Army for a short period, but he never spoke of his time there. After the War, he worked at Insley Manufacturing in Indianapolis, Indiana. He started at the very bottom and worked his way up to eventually become the manager of Parts & Services. The company held patents for cable-operated digging equipment such as Dragline excavators and power shovels, though they primarily made excavators used for digging in new building construction.

Howard was with the company for years and travelled often; the company sent him all over the United States, calling on the different shops that used and sold Insley parts. He could tell every customer what they needed, down to the very number of each part. The only state he never made it to was Hawaii. He was even sent to Alaska during the building of the Alaskan Pipeline, which occurred between 1974 and 1977.

The company once paid for Carolyn to visit him there, though she wasn't allowed to go to the pipeline itself because it was "top-secret". She did rent a car and travelled all around, touring the cities of Anchorage, Valdez and Fairbanks during her stay.

The Trans-Alaska Pipeline System (TAPS) includes the trans-Alaska crude-oil pipeline, 12 pump stations, several hundred miles of feeder pipelines, and the Valdez Marine Terminal. The pipeline is one of the world's largest pipeline systems, and the project attracted and employed tens of thousands of workers. It created a "boomtown" atmosphere in Anchorage at the time.

Carolyn and Howard had many years of happiness together while living in Indianapolis. They raised three children and had friends who were all married with children the same ages. After their children had been raised and were off living on their own, a new opportunity presented itself.

One of Howard's many business trips was set for Houston, Texas, and there he received an offer from a place he'd frequently called upon. The company wanted him to be their Parts & Services Director and offered him a job with more money and better benefits. Though the couple had lived their whole lives in Indianapolis, Carolyn said, "Why not? The kids are all gone now, so let's do something different." And that's what they did.

As for Carolyn's unfortunate turn of events, one day she and her husband were walking down the street in Texas, and she saw her reflection in the mirror. She noticed how crooked her body looked and asked Howard about it. He cheerfully replied, "No, honey, you are beautiful just the way you are", and she let it go.

It wasn't until a few years later, when they moved to South Carolina and she saw the medical report that had been sent from her doctor in Texas, when she first saw the word "scoliosis". Her doctor there had been a good friend, yet he never said anything about her condition, even though she'd undergone two back operations during her thirties and forties. A friend in Charleston looked up the word Carolyn saw on that report, then showed her the printout identifying the effects of scoliosis... many of them she'd already suffered. "I still have that paper he gave me, even after all these years," Carolyn shared with a look of sadness.

Carolyn still smiled when asked about her life and said she looks back with fondness. On her first date with Howard, she recalled with a smile, she'd ordered a chocolate soda and he ordered strawberry. Every year after, they celebrated on May 21st by finding a place that served ice cream, chocolate or strawberry syrup, and whip cream, reliving that first date.

They had a wonderful marriage; years ago a local newspaper featured an article about their love story that started in a soda shop in 1945. It was with Howard that Carolyn first saw the ocean, and they often went to Sanibel Island which was like a dream-come-true. She loved to collect shells, and many of those keepsake shells are treasured in two glass lamps in her room at Summit Place. She also loved to cook and bake, and when she and her husband made their final move to South Carolina, they made many new friends and threw tons of parties with them.

When Howard became sick in 2001 and needed an operation, he went to MUSC in Charleston for his treatment, yet less than a year later, the love of Carolyn's life passed away. Her father had died of cancer years before, and her mother passed away from old age a few years after, so those few years proved to be very difficult times. Today, her sister and her brothers are all gone, as well.

Of Carolyn's three children, Diane lives nearby in Summerville, South Carolina and works at the Mills House Hotel in Charleston as the Executive Housekeeper. David is a retired salesman for Porsche and writes stories; he lives in Wisconsin and has twin daughters and a son. The third child, Michael, recently died from cancer.

Last year, Carolyn's son David gave her a wonderful and welcomed surprise. He returned to their family home in Indianapolis on a fact-finding trip. He and his wife stopped at all the places Carolyn knew; her grade school and her husband's mother's home, to name a few. David took dozens of pictures and sent them to Carolyn. Though she mourns the loss of her husband and family who've gone, she said it was such a delight to see those wonderful images from her past that have always stayed close to her heart.

Williamsburg, South Carolina - February 1923

Mabel (Joy) Ward

Mabel Ward was born and lived in Williamsburg, South Carolina in the Kingstree county seat. Her father, Acue Joye, worked in the trucking business. He owned a large truck that he used for moving and hauling. Tobacco often filled the truck during the high season, while he hauled local farmers' tobacco batches from their farms to warehouses. Mabel's mother, Irene Joye, had taught school in a one-room schoolhouse in Georgetown County until she married.

After marriage and having children, Mabel's mother served as a twenty-four nurse in town, despite not being a registered midwife or a nurse with any formalized training. If anyone became ill, even in the middle of the night, the family would come get Irene so she could attend to them. Mabel said her mother's help was needed often enough that she never knew when her mother would leave home.

Mabel was the youngest of the family and a 'surprise' baby born during the Depression. She had one sister, Helen, older by twenty years, and two brothers in between, Haskell and Stoll. She was closest with Stoll, because Haskell ran away from home when he was just sixteen; he desperately wanted to fight in the war (World War II), so he joined the Marines down in Parris Island near Beaufort, South Carolina. When he got into some local trouble, their father had to go to Beaufort and give permission for Haskell to remain in the Marines, given his age as a minor.

Parris Island was first discovered by Europeans in 1562 when members of a French expedition led by Jean Ribaut temporarily settled on the island. It is perhaps best known for its United States Marine Corps training facility where about 16,000 Marines pass through boot camp every year. When asked about her childhood, Mabel said:

> "We grew up poor during the Depression, but everyone was poor. We didn't know, because we were all in the same boat. I remember when I was in grammar school, I loved to read, and we had a teacher who lived nearby. She'd let the neighbor kids borrow her books, and I read everything I could get my

hands on. Grace Livingston Hill was my favorite author, but I think I read every book that teacher had."

Mabel's brother, Haskell, was then sent to fight for his country in the Okinawa Islands in Japan, just as he'd hoped. Okinawa with an area of 1,200 square kilometers is made up of a few dozen, small islands in the southern half of the Nansei Shoto island chain. The Battle of Okinawa, code-named "Operation Iceberg," was the largest amphibious assault in the Pacific during WWII; an 82-day long battle that occurred from April to June in 1945.

The goal for the United States was to capture and control the strategic islands along a path toward the Japanese home islands and bring U.S. bombers within range for a possible invasion. However, the Japanese soldiers fought the island landings fiercely and killed many Allied soldiers, sometimes making desperate, last-ditch suicidal attacks. On Okinawa alone, during the eighty-two days of combat, approximately 100,000 Japanese troops and 12,510 Americans were killed.

On a Sunday night in the States, the famous producer, director and actor Orson Welles (1915 - 1985) aired a short documentary of a suicide bombing on Okinawa and the Marines who died there. Irene, Mabel's mother, had been watching the film, and she immediately thought her son had been killed. With her high blood pressure condition, the scare from the broadcast caused her to have a stroke then-and-there.

Though Haskell did return from the war almost a year later, healthy and unharmed, Irene was never the same. After her stroke, she needed constant help and care. As Mabel's older siblings got married and moved out, Mabel was left to take care of their mother. Mabel attended just seven months of her final year of high school in the eleventh grade, before having to leave and take care of her mother full-time. Note: It wasn't until eight years later, in 1948, when the twelfth grade would be added to high schools in South Carolina.

This was the same year the polio disease broke out in South Carolina. When polio came into town, isolation of infected families was the immediate solution. All community events were cancelled, children were confined to their homes, and even during the hottest days of summer, pools were closed. Schools and camps were shut down, movie theaters were closed, and drinking fountains were abandoned. People were forbidden from having any social gatherings in the communities.

Mabel witnessed this scare and paranoia first-hand, and the memory stayed with her. Though school had been closed, her high school, along with many others around the country, simply handed out the students' certifications of graduation on their last day of school and there was no formal ceremony to acknowledge the students' completion; essentially, no place where people could congregate and potentially spread the polio disease.

Mabel's family had lived in the country, then after she finished high school, they moved to a little town called Hemingway, South Carolina. She took a few business courses but did not attend college. She worked all during the years of the war; one job was as a clerk in the shoe department at Triber department store. The store was owned and operated by a Jewish family who had been told after the bombing of Pearl Harbor, "Leather purchasing is frozen, due to limited supply", which meant stores were not allowed to sell their shoes. However, Mabel's boss did not relay this information to her, and she continued to work and sell customers shoes. It wasn't long before the sheriff of Florence County issued warrants on the store, "and the Tomlinson department store across the street that didn't want to be outsold by its competition".

During the war, it wasn't only leather rationed in the United States, but gasoline and many other items. In May of 1942, after Pearl Harbor, the U.S. Office of Price Administration (OPA) froze prices on everyday goods including sugar and coffee. War ration books and tokens were issued, dictating how much gasoline, tires, sugar, meat, silk, shoes, nylon and other items any one person could buy, based on the number in each household.

> "During the war, we were issued books of stamps and only allowed to buy one or two pairs of shoes a year, on account of the leather. The military needed leather not just for the servicemen's shoes, but also for the fighter bomber jackets, so leather was rationed during those years."

One night after work, one of Mabel's good friends brought a boy to her house to see if she would like him, and she absolutely did. He lived about five miles away, in

Johnsonville; his name was John "Carroll" Taylor. The two dated for about two years and became very serious before finally deciding to marry. She was 20 years old when she called her siblings and told them it was time for her to have her own life, after living home and taking care of their mother those previous many years. Their mother went to live with one of her brothers, Stoll, who essentially offered because he knew it would keep him from having to go into the service.

> "After we got married, Carroll and I moved to Charleston where my sister and her husband had already moved. Carroll got a job working at a station, retreading tires. He had to go to school to learn the trade, because he'd been employed at Santee Electric before then. He wasn't drafted into the War because he had a heart condition. When he went to sign up, they issued him a "4-F" card on account of it."

About thirty percent of all registrants were rejected for physical defects after the WWII draft was instituted in 1940. The 4-F classification was given primarily for muscular and bone malformations, hearing or circulatory ailments, mental deficiency or disease, hernias, and syphilis. There were ramifications when a man was given that classification as well, because some women would look at them differently and think if a man wasn't fit for war, then he couldn't be fit for them.

Mabel didn't think twice, though, she was so smitten by Carroll. Not long after they were married, Mabel had to go back home to help take care of her ailing mother. Carroll was at work that day and asked Mabel if he should follow her home the next day. Though her childhood home wasn't far, because of the rationing, she told him she would be fine and to stay at home.

The next day, he and three friends went fishing at Santee Lake. It was in March, and it was so windy, their boat capsized. One man drowned, and though Carroll and his brother made it to shore, they had been in the water for too many hours and died. They had only held onto the boat too long to try to help the fourth guy who couldn't swim; ironically, he was the only one who survived the incident.

To compound the loss of her new husband and her mother, Mabel had already learned that she was expecting a baby; she delivered a boy four months later and named him after his father. She moved in with her sister and was hired for a six-month duration at the Naval yard in North Charleston — an office with over a hundred girls working in it and not a single man during the war. Her sister watch Mabel's son while she worked. One day she came home, and her sister exclaimed, "You'll never believe who came to see you today!" It was the boy she knew before she met Carroll. But Mabel was still mourning and told her sister and him she wasn't interested in dating.

> "I'd already had plans that night with a friend anyway, but that David Ward pursued me and soon we did start dating. I finally decided, I wanted a real home for my little boy, so David and I got married. We lived in Georgetown, South Carolina. He was working for International Paper Company, then."

"I'd told David before we were even married that I would never agree to having another child after the pain I'd experienced in losing Carroll. After two years, though, I changed my mind, and David and I had a baby girl. Joye Lynn was beautiful, and now she comes to see me every day. I don't know what I would have done without her."

Mabel's second husband, David, was transferred with his job to Winnsboro, South Carolina when Joye Lynn was just a few years old. "The kids had never seen snow until we moved there," she recalled. Mabel took a job as a teller at the local Savings & Loan Bank because her husband said if she wanted to buy the kids all the clothes she wished, then she needed to earn money. She later took a job at the Manhattan Shirt Company as Personnel Director and stayed with them for 15 years before eventually retiring.

Long after the children left home and soon after Mabel and David retired, they began to travel. They first went to

Hawaii, then to Europe - London, England, Scotland, Wales and Ireland. They visited the site where the Sound of Music was filmed on location in Salzburg, Austria. Finally, they went to Germany and up into the Alps of Switzerland.

They also visited Kehlsteinhaus, Adolf Hitler's place on the mountain known in English-speaking countries as "the Eagle's Nest". The Kehlsteinhaus is a Third Reich-era edifice erected atop the summit of the Kehlstein, a rocky outcrop rising above the Obersalzberg, near the town of Berchtesgaden. It was presented to Hitler on his 50th birthday as a retreat and place to entertain friends and visiting dignitaries. Today, the Eagle's Nest is open seasonally as a restaurant, beer garden, and tourist site.

In the States, the couple flew to Texas to see the "Alamo" - the Mission San Antonio de Valero, named for St. Anthony of Padua and built by Spanish settlers on the banks of the San Antonio River around 1718 - and then to California to see the redwood forests. Together, the couple enjoyed many good years before David suffered a severe stroke in 1989. Sadly, he never spoke another word again.

Though he lived until 2007, David spent his remaining years in a nearby Veteran's Hospital and required round-the-clock care. Fortunately, he was eligible for VA benefits because he had served in the War in the army for four years, before he'd met Mabel. He'd been in the Medical Corp and was sent to the Pacific, though like most of the men in his day, he rarely ever talked about his overseas experience.

"I travelled back and forth to see David

every day for more than a decade until I no longer could. I loved my first husband so much, but David was a good husband, too. And he was good to my son, Carroll. David always treated him as his own.

"A few times, David asked if he could adopt Carroll. But I wanted Carroll to carry on his father's name. In all, David and I had almost twenty years together before his stroke hit. We had a good life together."

Mabel and David's son attended Clemson and now lives in Chester, South Carolina. He has his own business as a forester, buying and selling timber. Joye, Mabel and David's daughter, went to the University of South Carolina; Joye now lives on Daniel Island, near Mabel. Mabel looks back on her life, her loves and family with great fondness.

Richmond, Kentucky - September 1925

Anthony "Tony" James

Anthony "Tony" James was born in Richmond, Kentucky, a city named after Richmond, Virginia, and the third-largest city in the Bluegrass region following Louisville and Lexington. Tony's parents had always told him he was born on the twenty-eighth of September, which is, of course, when they celebrated his birthday.

However, many years later, when he requested a state certificate, the official document stated his birthday to be the thirtieth. "When I asked my mother about it, she just laughed and told me they were wrong," Tony recalled.

He had ten brothers and sisters, with twenty years between the oldest and youngest child. The family lived on a farmhouse about ten miles outside of town until Tony was ten years old, then they moved to the center of town. The move wasn't by choice, though. One Sunday morning, their farm caught on fire while they were at church, and it burned to the ground. "We went to church, and when we came home, our house was gone. That was the end of it."

His father, John James, was of German descent. He was a farmer who traded cattle between stockyards from town-to-town. Their family didn't have much money, yet John James always made sure he had a smokehouse full of meats to feed the family.

There was another, less fortunate family who lived about a half mile down the road, and one especially hard season it was rumored that they had no meat or food to put on the table. So one of Tony's oldest brothers stole a ham without telling their father and gave it to the father. "He only took a ham because they had a girl his age, he was swell on," Tony grinned, "We didn't confess to our daddy what he had done until many years later, when he could no longer do anything about it."

Their mother, Dovie, was a sweet woman and a wonderful cook. Tony remembers how she was always doing something around the house to take care of their family.

"I think our mother liked the youngest kids the best. She was mighty good in the kitchen, though. We didn't have room at the table for us all, so my younger brother and I always had to sit on the bench to eat meals. About once a month, she'd make something called a Christmas cake, which was a big ole' fruit cake, as a treat for us. She actually cooked it in a small washing tub over the fire. We loved it, and it would last us for days.

"As for our schooling, we had to walk two miles back-and-forth from school every day. I had a good time in school, but in those days just getting to school was tough. They didn't have busses or after-school programs like they do now.

"Hell, they didn't even have an inside bathroom. It was outside in the backyard; the boys had one and the girls had their own. No, all the grades were together in one school, though there were two buildings. And somehow, I became the teacher's pet. I don't know how, but I surely was."

Tony was just a few months into the tenth grade when the Army took him out of school for the War. They sent him to California for his training, then onto New York. It was on New Year's Day of 1945 when he left New York City on the Queen Mary, sent to battle.

Since her maiden voyage nine years before, the Queen Mary had been the grandest ocean liner in the world. It carried Hollywood celebrities such as Bob Hope and Clark Gable, royalty with the Duke and Duchess of Windsor, and foreign dignitaries such as Winston Churchill. She even set a new speed record on the water, which she held for fourteen years.

However, when the Queen Mary docked in New York in September of 1939, that would be the last time for many years she would carry civilian passengers for pleasure. On that maiden war voyage in 1945, there were nearly 16,000 troops on board, with 18-20 men in each stateroom who slept in shifts day-and-night. There wasn't enough room for them all in the dining room, either, so they ate meals in shifts around the clock.

The Queen Mary's transformation into a troopship was an impressive one. For WWII, she was transformed, from a luxury ocean liner to a camouflaged ship that served the U.S. military for five years. She was painted a camouflaged grey color and stripped of her luxurious amenities. Dubbed the "Grey Ghost" because of her stealth and stark color, the Queen Mary was the largest and fastest troopship to sail. She was capable of transporting up to 16,000 troops at a time at a speed of thirty knots and made many trips back and forth across the Atlantic Ocean.

After WWII ended, the ship underwent a ten-month retrofitting process to return it to her original glory. On July 21, 1947, the Queen Mary resumed regular passenger service across the Atlantic and continued to do so for nearly two more decades. Today, the boat is now anchored off the port in Long Beach, California for public display.

For Tony's passage across the Atlantic and each new wave of troops, the Queen Mary landed in Gourock, Scotland. The trip took about five days from port-to-port. Tony's division was sent to England, where they then headed across the English Chanel in LST (Landing Ship Tank) ships into the combat zones. LST is the naval designation for vessels created during World War II to support amphibious operations by carrying vehicles, cargo, and landing troops onto unimproved shores.

Tony fought in many battles throughout Germany and France; his luck eventually ran out in Belgium. When he suffered a gunshot wound, the Army sent him to Paris to recover in an Army Hospital located not far from the Eiffel Tower. There, he received the Purple Heart for his service. The Purple Heart is a United States military medal awarded in the name of the President to those wounded or killed, while serving with the U.S. military; the medal has been issued to soldiers since April of 1917. Tony recalls this about the war:

"I got shot just because of some sneaky Germans. They'd captured a bunch of American uniforms and put them on. So, when my troop approached them, we were exposed out in an open field, and we didn't know they were Germans until it was too late. When they took fire on us, we hid behind some hills. We were lucky none of us died, and only two got shot. I was one."

When Tony returned home from the war, he didn't go back to finish his schooling, but stayed in the army for another two years. When asked if he had any humorous stories from his army days, he laughed and said this:

"Well, me and Tom, one of my buddies who'd been a personal friend for a long time, I went into the Army, but he went into the Navy. And when I was stationed in San Francisco, he called me one night and told me his ship was docked right off shore. Said he was coming ashore to see me.

"Well, we soon figured out that we had almost a hundred bucks between us, so Tom suggested that we go in town to pick up some girls. We went to the bars, found a couple of ladies with no problem, and bar-hopped with them for the night. Anyway, we had to be back at the barracks by 1 or 2am, but the girls said they were hungry, so we took them to this hole-in-the wall restaurant. That's when my buddy and I realized our money had run out.

"But Tom was quick, and he noticed that there

was just one gal working the restaurant. We all ate our food and then ran outta' there without paying. Tom held the door open at the front, and I threw her a quarter down on the counter, which is all we had left. That poor girl yelled at us something good, but we got away, and that was the end of it."

While Tony was stationed in England, he dated a young English girl. She wanted to come back with him and get married, but Tony didn't bring her because he already had a girl in the States whom he liked. Tony then said with a shrug, "Actually, there were two girls waiting for me. One of them was Dorothy, the girl I would marry. The other one... well, I can't even remember her name, now."

Dorothy was the sister of four brothers, and one of the guys had been friends with Tony. That friend told Tony he would bring his sister to meet him, but only once she graduated from high school. Tony said, he could still remember "just as plain as day" the first day he saw her walking across the street toward him. "I told her brother right then, he wasn't going to have a sister no more. I knew she was gonna' be my girl," Tony reminisced with a twinkle in his eye, and the couple married a month later. Dorothy was just out of high school and Tony was twenty-four years old.

When Tony had returned from the war, the army camp in Detroit is where he'd been discharged, so he and Dorothy stayed there for a number of years. They had three children, Michael, Donna and Stephen, and they all lived in Detroit for about ten years before they decided the city had become little too wild to raise a family.

They decided to move back to Kentucky, a state known as the "Bluegrass State" based on all of the bluegrass found in many of its pastures because of the fertile soil. Then they moved down to Fort Myers, Florida a few years later, "just to see what life in Florida was like". But Tony said this about their time there, "No one could speak English. You'd go to a restaurant, but you wouldn't know what you'd be ordering. We just didn't like it much there at all." While in Florida, Tony owned a Gulf station and Dorothy stayed home to take care of the children who were then still small. Though they enjoyed the beaches nearby, they'd finally had enough after five years and returned to Kentucky.

There they stayed for the remainder of the children's childhoods. Tony bought another small garage business and became an accomplished Volkswagen mechanic. He worked on VW cars and busses for from the mid-fifties until almost 1990 and loved his work. One of the greatest attributes of VW brand vehicles for many years was that the majority of the parts were interchangeable.

Tony became so adept at working on VW's that he could overhaul a car in just a day. As a VW enthusiast, Tony drove a '73 Super Beetle he'd overhauled before he stopped working. The color was dark blue ("Same as Kentucky colors, of course!") and is now kept in Charlotte where Tony's son, Michael, and his family live.

Volkswagen means "people's car" in German. In 1933, with many of the automobile projects still in development or early stages of production in Germany, Adolf Hitler got involved with the Volkswagen company. He wanted German citizens to have the same access to cars as Americans overseas, so he demanded the production of a basic vehicle, capable of transporting two adults and three children at 100 km/h (62 mph).

His vision was for this "People's Car" to become available to all citizens of the Third Reich through a savings plan, at 990 Reichsmark (RM) or $396 US dollars. Yet this amount was still too expensive for Germans as the average income was around 32RM per week. Erwin Komenda was the chief designer behind the now well-known "Beetle" car, which was eventually designed as an affordable vehicle for most everyone, around the globe.

Of their children, Michael graduated from Eastern Kentucky University where Dorothy had worked for ten years, in the University Bookstore. Donna attended for EKU a few years, as well, and currently lives in Mt. Pleasant. Their other son, Steve, followed in his father's footsteps with a love for cars and worked on them as a licensed mechanic (even if they weren't all VW's), until he died of cancer a few years ago.

All nine of Tony's siblings have passed away. The first was driving his truck when he had an accident that killed another man; he was so troubled, he committed suicide soon after, at thirty years old. The others have all passed away over the years from natural causes or diseases. And his last sibling died just three years ago, shortly after Tony's true love and childhood sweetheart, Dorothy, became ill and passed. Today, Tony is known as the "Candy Man" at Summit Place and always has a grin on his face. He has seen a lot in his life, experienced heartache and loss, yet his devil-may-care attitude and wonderful sense of humor are evident for all those who are near.

ACKNOWLEDGEMENTS

This writing project was a wonderful endeavor to undertake, and I want to wholeheartedly thank the Daniel Island Historical Society--in particular current President, Brenda Thorn, as well as Beth Bush and Lee Ann Bain--for their enthusiasm and support.

I also need to give a special thank you the staff at Summit Place, including Sean Davis, Executive Director, Chris Metts, at the front desk, Sheila Hutto who was a much-loved Activities Director at the facility for many years, and her counterpart, Diane Stewart, for their encouragement and assistance.

Finally, I extend warm and sincere gratitude to all the families who helped to make sure their loved one's stories were as factual as possible, and more importantly, for the stories to truly represent their long and amazing lives. Everyone was a delight to talk with to make this book happen.

ABOUT THE AUTHOR

Crystal began her career in executive sales and went on to earn a Masters degree in Healthcare Business, before turning to writing, teaching writing workshops, and full manuscript editing. Her love of story and a personal, family tragedy encouraged her to write her debut novel, Falling Through Trees, in the Kate Fox series. The second book, This Side of Perfect, picks up in the characters' lives one year after. The Days of Not So Long was another personal project that started with volunteer work at Summit Place.

She has also ghostwritten numerous family memoirs and has been a contributor for magazines including Daniel Island Life, the Occasions Guide, and What to Wear. She currently writes for the Falmouth/Cumberland Links in Maine.

Crystal lived in Kyiv, Ukraine, served as board president of the International Women's Club there, and has travelled extensively. She has created/taught numerous professional development classes stateside and overseas, and volunteers regularly with a heart for giving back.

From just outside of Portland, Maine, she continues to write dramatic stories and helps others develop and polish their own. She and her husband have two children and too many pets. You can read more and connect at www.CrystalColeBooks.com (pen name: Crystal Cole) or email her at crystalcolebooks@gmail.com.

www.ingramcontent.com/pod-product-compliance
Lightning Source LLC
Chambersburg PA
CBHW060155050426
42446CB00013B/2838